A School for Everyone

by the same authors

Emily Is Being Bullied, What Can She Do?
A Story and Anti-Bullying Guide for Children and Adults to Read Together
Helen Cowie, Harriet Tenenbaum and Ffion Jones
Illustrated by Ffion Jones
ISBN 978 1 78592 548 1
eISBN 978 1 78450 948 4

of related interest

Character Toolkit for Teachers
100+ Classroom and Whole School Character
Education Activities for 5- to 11-Year-Olds
Frederika Roberts and Elizabeth Wright
Foreword by Kristján Kristjánsson
ISBN 978 1 78592 490 3
eISBN 978 1 78450 879 1

Being Me (and Loving It)
Stories and Activities to Help Build Self-esteem, Confidence,
Positive Body Image and Resilience in Children
Naomi Richards and Julia Hague
ISBN 978 1 84905 713 4
eISBN 978 1 78450 236 2

Can I Tell You About Compassion?
A Helpful Introduction for Everyone
Sue Webb
Illustrated by Rosy Salaman
ISBN 978 1 78592 466 8
eISBN 978 1 78450 848 7

A SCHOOL FOR EVERYONE

Stories and Lesson Plans to Teach
Inclusivity and Social Issues

Ffion Jones, Helen Cowie and Harriet Tenenbaum

Illustrated by Ffion Jones

Jessica Kingsley Publishers
London and Philadelphia

First published in Great Britain in 2022 by Jessica Kingsley Publishers
An Hachette Company

1

Copyright © Ffion Jones, Helen Cowie and Harriet Tenenbaum 2022
Illustrations copyright © Ffion Jones 2022

Front cover illustration source: Ffion Jones.

A CIP catalogue record for this title is available from the
British Library and the Library of Congress

ISBN 978 1 78775 566 6
eISBN 978 1 78775 567 3

Printed and bound in Great Britain by CPI Group

Jessica Kingsley Publishers' policy is to use papers that are natural,
renewable and recyclable products and made from wood grown in
sustainable forests. The logging and manufacturing processes are expected
to conform to the environmental regulations of the country of origin.

Jessica Kingsley Publishers
Carmelite House
50 Victoria Embankment
London EC4Y 0DZ

www.jkp.com

Contents

Preface

This compendium of stories provides a resource that parents, teachers and other professionals who work with and care for children can use to address the everyday issues that preoccupy and worry young people. The book takes the form of stories, to be read to a group or a whole class, about individual children in one primary school class over the course of three terms. Each story is about one child's experience of a social or emotional concern; for example, being cyberbullied, being rejected, being targeted for being perceived as different, experiencing parental divorce or bereavement, worrying about appearance or gender, coming to the school from another country, being a refugee, living in poverty or having a parent in prison. For each issue, the story is followed by a fact file, a set of activities and a bank of resources to further enhance understanding. Activities can be selected based on the ages of the children involved. The aim of the compendium is to increase knowledge and understanding of each issue and to help children develop empathy for their peers who are experiencing such difficulties in their daily lives.

The Stories and Teacher Notes can be downloaded from
https://library.jkp.com/redeem using the code on p.155

Acknowledgements

We would like to acknowledge the help and guidance offered by the children and adults who read and critiqued earlier versions of this book. They include:

Alex Ayling, Anna Joseph, Isabel Barker, Lisa Cave (Greenpeace), Natasha Davies, Penny Davies, Ilias Diamantis, Olivia Dunn (Refugee Council), Judith Gentle, Kate Redruth, Ben Smith, Lauren Spinner, Louise Quinn-Flipping (National Autistic Society Swansea Branch), Millie Witcher and Erika Lye.

We would also like to thank James Cherry, Jessica Kingsley Publishers, and Emily Badger, for all her help.

AUTUMN TERM

1

Cyberbullying

How Does Jenny Deal with It?

Last year I was happy all the time – especially when I was with my best friend Yuki, who is from Japan. We used to walk my dog Patch on the common in all weathers. Sometimes we went back to my house to play computer games – the ones my mum and dad let me play!! Other times we went to Yuki's house. Her mum gave us lots of patterned silk material, which we made into dresses for our dolls. Last summer, though, Yuki's family had to go back to Japan. Before they left, Yuki sewed me a special pouch with silk pieces inside to clean my glasses with when they got steamed up. It was the best present I ever got in my life as it reminded me so much of her.

When term began, I was all on my own. At first, I didn't mind. But after a while I began to feel quite lonely, especially at break times. One day, Isla, Jade and Tamsin came up to me in the playground. I had never really liked them very much as they didn't ever want to play with Yuki and had said a few nasty things about her. But they seemed to want to be friends with *me*, so I began to hang out with them. They were always taking photos of each other on their mobiles and sharing them on Snapchat. That was fun at first until I noticed that they often posted horrible pictures of me and then laughed at them. In the summer I get loads of freckles, which mum calls "sun kisses," but they said my freckles looked like spots all over my face. They posted pictures of my feet looking enormous. They began to make nasty comments about my turquoise glasses. But all the time they said it was only in fun and I should learn to take a joke.

After school one day, we all went back to Jade's house. They opened up *Fortnite* on her computer. My heart sank because I'm not allowed to play that game. When I told them, they said I was such a baby. They carried on playing anyway so I felt very left out. I tried hard not to cry but my glasses all steamed up and when I took out my special pouch of silk squares to wipe them, Jade grabbed it.

"What a weird bag," she said. "Look at those awful colours! They don't even match!"

I dived onto Jade to snatch it back but the little pouch got torn in the scuffle. All the little silk squares fell to the floor. Jade stamped on them and then threw them up in the air so they scattered. I gathered up as much as I could and rang my mum to collect me as it was dark outside. By the time she arrived I had calmed down a bit. She asked if I was okay, but I didn't feel like talking about what had happened.

Next day at school, Isla, Jade and Tamsin kept talking about *Fortnite* so I couldn't join in. They said they were going to play it again after school but didn't invite me. That evening I got a message on my phone that said, "No one likes you Jenny. No wonder you're always on your own." I wasn't sure who had sent it as I didn't recognize the number, but I had a suspicion it was from Jade.

The following day, I found out that Isla had filmed me diving onto Jade to get my silk pouch back. I was screaming and shouting and looked dreadful, with a red face, glasses twisted to the side, my long red hair in a tangle and tears streaming down my face. Isla, Jade and Tamsin kept playing the video and laughing. Then Tamsin threatened to send it round the whole class. I really believed that she would.

That evening I got more messages. They said that I was ugly and that everyone was laughing at me.

Next morning, I was so embarrassed that I just couldn't go to school in case everyone had seen the video. I felt angry with myself and very ashamed. I told my mum I had a bad headache and a very sore stomach. That evening, I was still upset.

"What is it?" Mum asked. "Is something upsetting you?"

I started to cry. Mum said, "You know you can always tell me when things go wrong."

That made me cry even more but, in the end, I said, "I really need to tell you something about what's been happening at school." And it all came out. Although I cried a lot as I told her, it was better than having all those horrible feelings bottled up inside me. As we spoke, my phone pinged and another message came up that said, "You are a loser!"

Mum said, "The first thing we have to do is block that anonymous user!" and she showed me how to do it. "The next thing I am going to do is to ring Mrs Davies."

I didn't want Mum to tell Mrs Davies at first, but then I realized it had to be stopped before it got any worse.

The next day, Mrs Davies held a group meeting with Isla, Jade and Tamsin as well as me, Hind and Jamie and some other nice children from the class, and she told us that what had happened is called cyberbullying. Luckily, Tamsin *hadn't* posted the video. They all said that it was just in fun and that they meant no harm and it wouldn't happen again. I didn't believe them, but after that the cyberbullying stopped. During the group meeting Jamie said that he'd had a problem with cyberbullying too. Hind said that when she first came to the school she felt very left out and often felt like crying. Afterwards, Jamie and Hind asked if I would like to play with them. I also found that some other people in the class wanted to be friends with me.

It was hard to tell Mum my problem and it was hard to talk about it in the group, but afterwards I felt so much better, especially when I could see that I was not the only person to be cyberbullied. Mrs Davies told me how important it was to talk about your problems *only* with someone you can trust. She also held some lessons for the whole class on *netiquette*, which is all about behaving well and politely online.

That evening, Mum told me that she had arranged a Skype call with Yuki for the weekend. I was so excited. I told Yuki a bit about the cyberbullying and then she told me that she had found it very hard going back to school in Japan as she had been away for a whole year. She said that, at first, she was left out by the others in her class, who had all made their own friends. She told me that in Japan they call bullying *ijime*, so I realized that I am definitely not the only one to have been affected by it. It's happening all over the world. When I showed her the silk pouch all crumpled and torn, she looked very sad for me and said, "Please don't worry about it." Two weeks later a parcel came for me from Japan. Inside was a new silk pouch even more beautiful than the last one.

TEACHER'S NOTES

Lesson objectives

◇ To introduce pupils to the issue of bullying and cyberbullying and facilitate discussion about the emotional impact on the target child, on the child who bullies and on the bystanders.

Fact file

Traditional bullying is usually defined as:

1. Repeated aggression towards someone who cannot easily defend themselves.

2. A systematic abuse of power.

Cyberbullying is usually defined as:

1. An aggressive, intentional act carried out by an individual or group, using mobile phones or the internet, repeatedly and over time against a victim who cannot easily defend themselves.

2. It is also a systematic abuse of power through; for example, the bullies' knowledge of ICT skills and their ability to hide their online identity.

3. It tends to be indirect rather than face to face.

4. The breadth of the potential audience is larger than with traditional bullying and the variety of bystander responses tends to be more complex.

Some researchers, including Bauman (2013), suggest calling it *cyber-aggression* rather than *cyberbullying*.

Cyberbullying includes such behaviour as:

◇ attacks and threats

◇ put-downs

◇ flaming (online verbal fights)

◇ intimidation online

◇ social exclusion (e.g. from an online group)

◇ masquerade (pretending to be someone else)

◇ outing (sharing information that was given to you in confidence)

◇ distributing embarrassing photos/videos of another person.

Research studies of cyberbullying report different rates, depending on the age of the child, the ways in which cyberbullying is defined and the frequency of the cyberbullying (e.g. "just once or twice" or "once a week or more often"). Occasional or "one-off" occurrences are reported by around 20 per cent of children and young people, but serious, persistent cyberbullying affects around 5 per cent; that is, less than for traditional bullying.

Research studies identify several characteristics typical of cyberbullies:

1. *Lack of empathy* for the distress that their actions cause. In the story, Jade, Tamsin and Isla showed no concern for Jenny's feelings during the bullying episodes.

2. *Moral disengagement.* This is a process through which someone can bypass the reasoning that holds us back from hurting another person. Bullies often justify their actions by such rationalizations as "He deserved it as he was annoying" or "It was only a joke." In the story, Jade, Tamsin and Isla continued to maintain that their actions were only done for fun and showed little remorse during the group meeting.

3. *Machiavellianism.* This is a form of cold, manipulative behaviour as well as a sense of entitlement and superiority to the victim. Jade, Tamsin and Isla enjoyed taunting Jenny and damaging her precious possession. They also got pleasure out of winding her up so that she became emotionally out of control.

Help and support for children and young people

There are many charities, organizations and government agencies concerned with the mental health of children and young people, such as Childline, the Anti-Bullying Alliance, Barnardo's, YoungMinds and The Diana Award, which provide useful resources for the prevention and reduction of cyberbullying, as well as guidance for parents and teachers. In the UK some key legislation determines how bullying is to be dealt with in schools. Every state-funded school must have measures in place to prevent all forms of bullying among pupils. In the case of cyberbullying, which often takes place outside school hours, the Education and Inspections Act (2006) gives head teachers the power to discipline pupils for poor behaviour that occurs even when the pupil is not on school premises. Consequently, incidents that occur on the journey to and from school or in cyber space can be disciplined by the relevant authority at school. Though bullying is not in itself a crime, some forms of harassing or threatening behaviour could be a criminal offence. For example, revenge porn was made a criminal offence under the Criminal Justice and Courts Act 2015, which made it illegal to share sexual images or videos without the consent of the person involved.

In the story, Jenny was vulnerable when her best friend, Yuki, went back to Japan. She then became an easy target for Isla, Jade and Tamsin, who enjoyed watching her emotional distress and threatening her with further humiliation. Her immediate reaction was to keep her shame and embarrassment to herself. It was understandable that she would find it difficult to share her experience of cyberbullying with anyone. But through telling someone she trusted, initially her mum, she experienced an immediate sense of relief. Mrs Davies built on this by using one of the many strategies available to schools, in this case *The Support Group Method*, to facilitate a dialogue among the girls who carried out the cyberbullying and their target, Jenny, in the supportive context of a wider peer group. She then reinforced this message by holding a series of lessons with the whole class about staying safe online and using the internet wisely.

Comprehension activities

1. How did Jenny feel when Yuki had to return to Japan with her family?

2. Why do you think that she tried to be friends with Isla, Jade and Tamsin when she hadn't really liked them very much before?

3. Why did Isla, Jade and Tamsin see Jenny as a target for cyberbullying?

4. Why was it so difficult for Jenny to tell anyone about being cyberbullied?

5. What is *netiquette* and why is it important?

Further activities

1. Trust-building exercise: Introduce Your Neighbour. The teacher gives the class five questions that they need to ask their neighbour (the person sitting beside them). They should be factual questions, for example, about hobbies, but nothing too personal. They can be amusing or unusual. Nothing is written down. Each partner is asked to remember what their neighbour tells them. They then present their partner to the whole group based on the information they have gathered.

2. What can the bystander do? In small groups, on large cards, write down ways in which bystanders could help a classmate who is being cyberbullied. Each suggestion gets a separate card. If you like, illustrate each suggestion with a drawing. Each group puts their cards up on the wall and presents them in turn to the whole class. Suggestions that are similar are grouped together. The whole class discusses the strengths and any potential difficulties of each type of action.

3. Force-field analysis. The class divides into pairs. One person identifies an issue about themselves that they would like to change. (The teacher reminds the class that it is not a good idea to begin with a very sensitive issue.) For example, Jane says, "I am not very confident at sport. I wish I could change that." Her partner, Amy, helps her to work on the issue using *Force-field analysis*. First, she draws an arrow-shaped line towards the issue "I want to be more confident at sport." She then helps Jane to draw the forces that prevent her from being more confident. Each force has a separate line going down at right angles to the original arrow. Then Jane helps Amy to identify the strengthening forces that could help her to achieve her goal. These are drawn as lines going up at right angles to the arrow. The longer the line, the stronger the force. Once the diagram has been drawn, the pair discuss how to put an action plan together by decreasing the hindering forces and increasing the helping forces.

HELPING FORCES

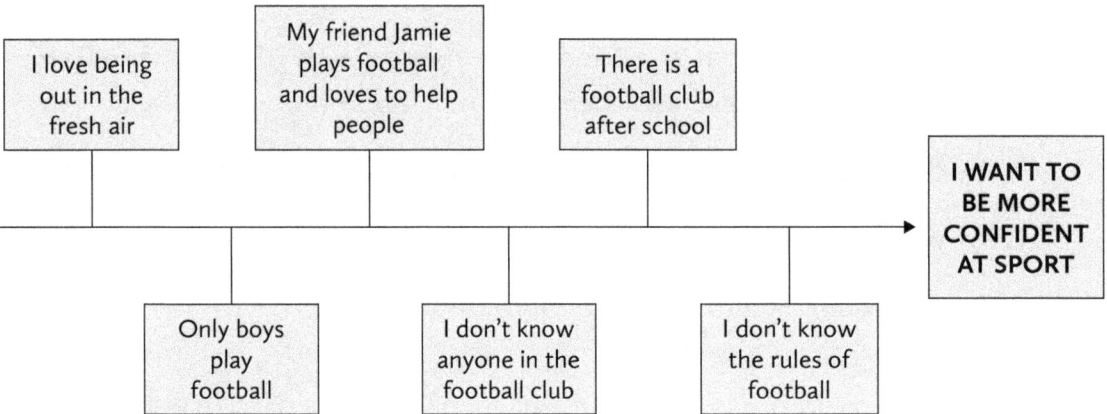

UNHELPFUL FORCES

4. Role play. Someone in your class has sent you a nasty text message. You are really upset as you do not know who it is, though you have some suspicions. You decide to tell your very best friend. Role play what happens when you do this. Your friend makes some suggestions about how to solve the problem. Change places and reverse the roles. Finally, present the solutions to the whole class.

> **Teacher's note** – Ensure that everyone de-roles after the activity.

RESOURCES

Article

Bauman, S. (2013) "Cyberbullying: what does research tell us?" *Theory into Practice*, 52(4): 249–256.

Websites

Anti-Bullying Alliance www.anti-bullyingalliance.org.uk/tools-information/all-about-bullying/online-bullying/cyberbullying-and-law

> This site contains up-to-date information about cyberbullying and the law as well as a wide range of resources for children and young people as well as for parents and teachers.

Blurred Lives www.ou.nl/web/blurred-lives/project

> This is a European project that focuses specifically on cyberbullying. Its brief is to cover school policies, anti-bullying materials, teacher training materials for anti-bullying work, guidance for parents, and guidance for children and young people.

Ditch The Label https://us.ditchthelabel.org

> The aim of this international organization is to provide up-to-date resources and research findings to support children who are being bullied. They have useful resources on both offline and digital communities.

The Metropolitan Police http://safe.met.police.uk/index.html

> The London Metropolitan Police service has a website that informs children and young people about crime and safety issues that concern them, including bullying and cyberbullying.

The National Society for the Prevention of Cruelty to Children (NSPCC) https://learning.nspcc.org.uk/child-abuse-and-neglect/bullying

> The NSPCC has useful definitions of bullying/cyberbullying and a range of resources to help children understand what is happening and take appropriate action.

The Support Group Method www.education.vic.gov.au/about/programs/bullystoppers/Pages/methodsupportgroup.aspx

> The Support Group Method is a non-punitive intervention strategy. This method gathers assistance for the victimized student. It does this by sharing knowledge of their distress at a meeting with the perpetrators, together with peers who would offer support to the victim.

UK Safer Internet Centre www.saferinternet.org.uk

> This site offers tips and guidance for children and young people on how to stay safe online. It also organizes conferences and provides teaching resources.

Wise Kids https://wisekids.org.uk/wk/cyberbullying

> This site has very useful advice for children and teachers about the issue of cyberbullying.

Youthworks https://youthworksconsulting.co.uk

> This site provides useful information about bullying and cyberbullying. It specializes in accessing children's views, especially on their digital experience.

2

Becky and Her Frenemies

I couldn't wait for the first day back at school. The end of the holidays is always so boring and I had some exciting news to tell Yasmin and Niamh.

"Guess what!" I squealed, when I saw them at the gates. "I've been chosen to dance in Snow White!"

I'd been going to dance club for ages and it was first time I'd been chosen to be in the Christmas Pantomime. I was so excited!

"No way!" said Yasmin, jumping up and down with a big smile on her face. "That's so cool!"

I looked over at Niamh, who seemed a bit annoyed. After a while, she glanced at me with raised eyebrows. "If that's the kind of thing you like then great," she said. "But I wouldn't want to be in it myself. It probably means you have to miss out on loads of parties because of all the rehearsals. And I'm all about the party, girls!"

We all laughed but I suddenly felt embarrassed about being so excited.

"Yeah, you're right," I said. "I hadn't really thought about that."

I always ended up agreeing with Niamh even if I didn't really agree with her deep down. Ever since we were little she always put a damper on things I was excited about or called me out for bragging. She usually said she was just being "honest" or "saying it like it is." If I'm being honest though, it sometimes felt a bit mean and usually made me feel really bad.

With a big grin on her face, she nudged Yasmin, who was giggling nervously.

"Are you going to be one of the seven dwarves, then?" she laughed, saying it loud enough so that everyone walking past could hear too.

"Very funny," I said, though it didn't feel funny at all. Niamh came up with my nickname, "Shorty," in Year 1 and it kind of stuck. I'm not even that short really but I suppose I am one of the shortest girls in the class. No one knows that the nickname upsets me because I pretend I don't care. I think Niamh could tell I was upset this time though because I wasn't laughing it off like I usually do. I'd been wanting to do the panto for ages and I just wanted them to be excited for me.

"It's only a joke, Miss Sensitive," she said, dragging Yasmin away. "I wish you wouldn't take things so seriously all the time."

By the time we got to class, I'd decided it wasn't a big deal and that I shouldn't get so wound up. We've known each other forever so I should be used to her teasing by now. Maybe I was being too sensitive. I plastered a smile on my face and sat down next to Yasmin and Niamh. Mrs Davies said we had to get into pairs to create a poster of what we did over the holidays. I shuffled up to Yasmin and Niamh, but Niamh quickly grabbed Yasmin's arm and said "It's pairs, not threes."

I think Mrs Davies saw because she said it was okay if people wanted to work in threes.

"We're working in a pair, Becky," snapped Niamh. "We've got a play date tonight and we can finish the poster then, so you can't really be with us."

I know it sounds silly, but it felt like a punch to the stomach. Niamh was always doing this in class. I didn't understand why she was being horrible to me. I pretended I was okay and luckily Iliana, sitting behind me, didn't have a partner either. Iliana had heard about me being in the panto and said, "You should definitely put that on the poster because it's so exciting."

I didn't answer because I wasn't really concentrating. All I could think about was that Yasmin and Niamh had a play date, which meant that the rest of the day would be a nightmare. Whenever they had a play date, they'd go on about it all day, leaving me out of everything.

At lunch break they didn't even notice I was upset and sitting on my own because they were too busy talking about what they were going to do later. I looked over and Niamh glanced at me briefly, then turned her back and laughed. How could my best friends make me feel so bad? It was so confusing.

When I got home that night I was in such a bad mood that I snapped at Mum when she asked how my day had been.

"Someone's tired," she laughed. I thought she'd think I was just being silly if I told her why I was upset, so I pretended I *was* tired.

"Can Niamh come over for a play date tomorrow?" I asked. As upset as I was with Niamh, play dates always sorted it out because she'd be nice to me then for the whole day. It might sound weird but, even after she'd been mean, I still wanted to be her friend. I guess it's because I'd known her for so long and sometimes she could be really nice.

In school the next day, I ran over to Niamh and Yasmin, but they blanked me and turned away. They were whispering about what they'd done in their play date and laughing at some in-joke that I didn't understand. I had to go right up to them and wave before they even said hello to me and even then they were acting really weird.

"Mum says you can come over later, Niamh," I said.

"Yes!" she quickly turned to face me. "Your house is the BEST for play dates." I could see Yasmin's face drop.

Niamh grabbed hold of my arm and pulled me into the class, leaving Yasmin behind. She didn't leave my side all day. I told Yasmin to come and sit with us and that we could work together in a three, but Niamh kept whispering not to play with her. At lunch play, she pulled me to one side and said how boring it was at Yasmin's house. I felt uncomfortable and didn't know what to say so I laughed it off. She talks about everyone behind their back so I'm guessing she talks about me too, but I was just relieved that I wasn't being left out again.

After school, we had such a laugh in my house. Niamh can be hilarious. We spent most of the time in my room and she found my lock diary. No one's allowed to read it, but she promised she wouldn't tell anyone. She read out my "secret crush" page and then kept teasing me about Ben, who I really like.

"Becky and Ben sitting in the tree, K-I-S-S-I-N-G," she laughed.

It was pretty funny. I told her I wanted to keep it private and she said wouldn't even tell Yasmin.

When I arrived in school the next morning, Yasmin and Niamh and some of our other friends from class were all standing in a big group. When I started walking towards them, they all sniggered and looked at me.

"Here she is!" laughed Niamh. "How's lover boy Ben today?"

I knew straight away that she'd told everyone. I had to turn away because I was so upset.

"It's no big deal, Becky," Niamh said, when she saw I was tearing up. "No one cares anyway."

I cared, and it was a massive deal to me. I couldn't believe she'd broken her promise and told everyone. She was meant to be my friend and sometimes – quite a lot of the time actually – it didn't feel very friendly at all.

I ran off and hid in the toilets. After a while, Yasmin came to find me and told me not to worry because everyone would forget about it by next week. I was so embarrassed that I sat on my own for the rest of the day – not that Niamh seemed bothered.

The rest of the week was horrible. Yasmin and Niamh kept going off together and whispering and then they'd say it was a "private chat" when I'd come near them. I didn't have a clue whether they were laughing at me or not, but they kept looking over and giggling so it felt like they were. I felt so lonely and left out. In lessons they acted like nothing was wrong so I guess Mrs Davies didn't know I was upset. But then at playtimes they'd completely ignore me.

On Friday when I got home, I was so tired of it all that I burst into tears in front of Mum. It was so embarrassing. Mum usually wades in and tries to fix things, but I didn't want that. I took a deep breath and told her I just wanted her to listen. I explained what had been happening. It was such a relief because she seemed to understand and didn't think I was being silly. She said she understood how bad I was feeling because she'd gone through the same type of thing when she was in school.

"When it happened to me," she said, "I eventually plucked up the courage to tell my friends that I was upset. My real friends felt really bad and stopped and I realized that my other friends, who didn't say sorry, weren't really friends at all."

I knew what she was getting at, but I've known Niamh forever and she's in our group so I wasn't sure how that would work.

"You'll figure it out, love," Mum said. "And you can talk to me about it any time."

She also said I could arrange some play dates with some of my other friends, which I thought sounded good. I knew I had to do something after the week I'd had.

Even though I was really scared, when I got to school I asked Yasmin and Niamh for a chat. I was so nervous.

"I've been really upset that you keep leaving me out," I said. "And I know you think you're saying things in a joking way, but some of the jokes you make about me aren't really funny."

Niamh rolled her eyes and laughed. It felt like another punch to the stomach.

"Don't be so dramatic," she said. "Can't you take a joke?"

She starting to walk off, grabbing Yasmin's arm to come with her. But Yasmin pulled away.

"Becky, I'm so sorry," she said. "I don't want you to be upset. Sorry if we've left you out."

"Don't worry, Yasmin," I said. "Thanks for saying sorry." I gave her a massive hug, more relieved than anything. Niamh let out an angry sigh before storming off.

"Don't worry, she'll calm down," Yasmin said. "I really am sorry."

I sat with Yasmin and Iliana at lunch and it felt nice to have a laugh together. Niamh eventually came over and sat next to us, but she blanked me completely. Yasmin didn't join in though and carried on talking to me.

Me and Yasmin are still best friends and I'm really glad I gave her a second chance. I'm not close with Niamh anymore though. I was so sad to begin with because I've known her forever, but when she carried on ignoring me after I'd told her how I felt, I realized things could never get back to normal. Real friends, however long you've known them, don't talk about you behind your back or ignore you all the time. She's still in our group and we hang out sometimes, but we've drifted apart. I was worried at first that it would cause problems, but, after a while, I realized it's better this way. It's a relief not being the butt of someone's jokes all the time – Yasmin and Iliana laugh with me, not at me. I've also made loads of new friends in the panto rehearsals. It's nice being around people who make me feel good about myself.

TEACHER'S NOTES

Lesson objectives

- ◇ To help pupils to distinguish between true friends and friends who sometimes act like enemies (frenemies).

- ◇ To give pupils strategies to deal with frenemies and to encourage them to pursue healthy relationships and to stand up for themselves.

Fact file

A frenemy is a person who has the characteristics of a friend and an enemy. For example, they may be nice to the child's face but repeatedly talk about them behind their back or spread rumours and gossip. Alternatively, they might tease them to their face, say hurtful things to them or encourage others to laugh at them, and call it a "joke." They may be friendly one minute and then the next minute give them the "silent treatment" or leave them out. They often talk about play dates or activities in front of the child who is not invited. They don't make the child feel good about themselves but their manipulative behaviour is often subtle so children find it hard to put a finger on what they are experiencing. As frenemies alternate between kindness and aggression, the friendship dynamic can be very confusing for the child. Sometimes, the behaviour becomes so normalized that the child does not notice it anymore.

Identifying a frenemy and realizing that their behaviour is at fault is an important first step. Children can then be encouraged to let their frenemy know how their behaviour is making them feel. Depending on their response, the child can then decide if they want to end or maintain a friendship with them.

All friendships experience conflict. In the story, Becky and Yasmin experience conflict but work through their issues and remain friends. Children should be encouraged to recognize that conflict is a normal aspect of relationships. However, a healthy relationship, with normal levels of conflict, looks and feels very different from an unhealthy relationship with a frenemy. When a friend becomes a "frenemy," they are not acting like a true friend who respects and cares for them, and children should be encouraged to recognize the difference. In the story, Becky thinks about what real friendship means to her and lets her friendship with Niamh drift apart as she realizes that Niamh is not acting like a true friend. Initially she wants to be her friend, but she does not like the way she is being treated by her. She gives her a chance and tells her how she is feeling, but when things do not change she has the confidence to walk away. Children should be encouraged to think about what real friendship means to them and the values involved in maintaining healthy relationships. Once they know what this looks and feels like, it is easier to either walk away from unhealthy relationships or to try to change those relationships by being assertive and standing up for themselves when needed. Even if a child wants to maintain the friendship with their frenemy, they can be encouraged to walk away or to speak up when their friend is acting in a negative way. If they are able to recognize the negative behaviour for what it is, they are better equipped to deal with it when it happens. Children should also be encouraged to have a wide circle of friends in and out of school so they are not reliant on one particular person or group of friends. This will also help them to recognize what real friendship is.

Frenemies act negatively for a variety of reasons. Sometimes, it is because they get a certain reaction when they act in a negative way. If the child on the receiving end is taught not to react or to react in an assertive and confident way, the dynamic can start to shift. Sometimes, children who act like frenemies are from stressful, insecure or controlling backgrounds so they try to exert control within their own friendship groups. They may feel insecure so act in a negative way – forming cliques and excluding others – to hide these insecurities and assert their dominance so that they can feel socially powerful. While good friendships are equally balanced, frenemies like to have power and control over others. Once children can recognize these unacceptable behaviours, they can be taught strategies to stand up for themselves and take back control.

Comprehension activities

1. How do you think Becky was feeling when her friends kept leaving her out?

2. Why do you think her friends were leaving her out?

3. In the story, Becky asks why Niamh is being so "horrible" to her. Why do you think Niamh is being unkind?

> **Teacher's note** – Explain to the class that there could be many different reasons for her negative behaviour. For example, she could be jealous that Becky is in the pantomime or she may be hiding her own insecurities and making Becky feel bad to try to feel better about herself. We often do not know the reasons that children are unkind to each other. It is important to emphasize that Niamh's behaviour is not Becky's fault.

4. In the story, Becky laughs at some of Niamh's nasty comments about Yasmin. Why do you think she does this? What could she do instead?

5. How do you think Becky was feeling when she confronted her friends and told them how their behaviour towards her made her feel?

6. Do you think it was a good or bad idea for Becky to tell her friends how she was feeling?

7. Compare and contrast Yasmin and Niamh's responses when Becky tells them that their behaviour has upset her.

Further activities

1. Warm-up activity. Pupils to sit in a circle. Each pupil has to say a word that represents qualities of a good friendship (e.g. trust, kindness). If they hesitate or cannot think of a word, they are out of the game and it passes to the next person. The winner is the last person left in the game.

2. What are values? Working in pairs, write your own definition and feed back to the rest of the class.

3. What are the values that most matter to you in a friendship? What qualities do you look for in a friend? Draw an outline of a person and write down all these qualities inside the body outline, showing what makes a good friend.

4. What do you think a "frenemy" is? Working in pairs, write your own definition and feed back to the rest of the class.

5. Draw two separate columns on your page. In the left column, write down all the characteristics of a good friend and in the right column, write down all the characteristics of a "frenemy." Feed back to the rest of the class.

6. Make a list of character traits that make a good friend. Next to each trait write down what the behaviour that goes with that trait looks like.

7. Why do you think it is important to have good friendships? Discuss in small groups and feed back to the class.

> **Teacher's note** – Emphasize the link between good friendships and positive self-esteem and how this is a two-way thing – if we act in a positive way to others and they act in the same way to us, we all feel better about ourselves.

8. Write down three ways in which you are a good friend and three ways in which you could be a better friend.

9. Write a recipe for a "Friendship cake," using all the friendship "ingredients" we have discussed. Remember to use baking terminology (e.g. tablespoon, weight measurements, etc.).

> **Teacher's note** – The pupils should look at cookbooks for inspiration at the start of the lesson.

10. Design a poster to put up in the school showing how to be a good friend. Include all the characteristics, behaviours and values that make a person a good friend.

11. Draw around one member of the class on a large sheet of paper – tell the class that they are going to make this drawing into their "perfect friend." The class should contribute ideas on what they think makes the perfect friend. Think about all the positive qualities a friend should have. They write all these characteristics around the drawing to display in the classroom.

RESOURCES

Books
Fiction

Bowe, J. (2011) *My Best Frenemy (Friends for Keeps)*, reprint edition. London: Puffin Books.

Howe, C. (2018) *Ella on the Outside.* London: Nosy Crow.

Non-fiction

Alexander, P. and Goddard-Hill, B. (2018) *Create Your Own Happy*. London: HarperCollins.

Carey, T. (2019) *The Friendship Maze: How to Help Your Child Navigate Their Way to Positive and Happier Friendships*. London: Hachette.

Criswell, P.K. and Martini, A. (2013) *Friendship Troubles: Dealing with Fights, Being Left Out, and the Whole Popularity Thing*. Middleton, WI: American Girl Publishing.

Simmons, R. (2011a) *The Curse of the Good Girl: Raising Authentic Girls with Courage and Confidence*. London: Penguin.

Simmons, R. (2011b) *Odd Girl Out: The Hidden Culture of Aggression in Girls*, revised edition. New York: Mariner Books.

Thompson, M. and O'Neill, G. (2002) *Best Friends, Worst Enemies: Understanding the Social Lives of Children*. New York: Ballantine.

Way, N. (2013) *Deep Secrets: Boys' Friendships and the Crisis of Connection*. Cambridge, MA: Harvard University Press.

Websites

Kidscape www.kidscape.org.uk

> Kidscape provides children and families with information and advice about how to prevent bullying and keep children safe.

Raising Children https://raisingchildren.net.au/pre-teens/behaviour/peers-friends-trends/frenemies

> Raising Children has a useful section about frenemies and toxic friendships.

3

Niall Has Had a Family Bereavement

I was really nervous about going back to school. I kept worrying about how people would react when they found out about Dad. Would they ask me loads of questions? Would they not say anything at all? For everyone else it had been a normal summer holiday, but everything had changed for me. Even though Dad had been sick for a long time before the holidays, nothing can prepare you for your dad actually dying.

Even though I was nervous about going back, I was looking forward to it too. I thought being back in a routine might help me to get my mind off things and I figured school would be a break from everything – not just from thinking about Dad not being there anymore, but also from having to see Mum cry, which really sucked. At least at school there's other stuff to think about – even if it's boring school work!

Mrs Brace, my old teacher, helped with my nerves about going back. She phoned us at the end of the holidays and said, "I'm sorry to hear about your dad." I thought that was really nice because it showed she was thinking about us. She asked Mum if it was okay for her to visit us at home, which really helped too.

"What will help you?" she asked me, and then she talked about what my new teacher, Mrs Davies, could tell my class. I wanted to be treated normally but was worried about everyone whispering and looking at me weirdly. We both agreed that Mrs Davies telling everyone would make it easier because it meant I didn't have to. I was glad Mrs Davies already knew too so I didn't have to explain things again.

Mum helped me to write a letter for Mrs Davies to read out about what had happened and said I didn't have to be there when she read it out. Before Mrs Brace left, we talked about how I could answer questions from my classmates and she helped me to think about what to say if I didn't want to talk about things straight away. I felt better knowing I could just say, "I don't want to talk at the moment." I hoped my friends would understand.

On the first day back I went in a bit late and my best friends Henry and Felix met me in the office, which made it easier to go back to class. When I went in, Mrs Davies quietly said, "I'm so sorry to hear about your dad," and asked how I was doing. I was so glad she'd said something because Cara, my aunt, had visited the other day and had tried to act like nothing had happened. She didn't even mention Dad. Mum said Cara didn't want to upset me by bringing it up, but it made me more upset because it felt like she didn't care.

Mrs Davies had already read the letter out so everyone knew and a few people came over and asked if I was okay, which was nice. I'm guessing they'd seen Mrs Davies asking how I was so they did the same.

Being back at school is a relief because it's all normal there, which makes me feel a bit more normal. We're trying to get used to our new "normal" at home, but it's hard. Mum always says I'm being "really brave," but sometimes I don't feel brave. But there's days when she's so upset that I pretend I'm okay to make her feel better. When I'm at school it's like a break from that. I can talk to Mrs Davies or my old teacher without worrying about upsetting anyone. They're both really good at listening. I can also have a laugh with my friends at school without worrying. At home I try not to laugh too much because it doesn't seem right when Mum's so upset.

I've had a few problems at school though, especially if I've had a bad week and bottled things up. All these confusing feelings build up until it feels like my head's going to explode. I actually start to get a headache and then I can't concentrate. Mrs Davies lets me go and sit by the office, which helps, but I hate feeling like that. One minute I'm fine and then suddenly I get really angry. There's no way around it – I'm just really angry that Dad had to die. It seems so unfair. When you start thinking like that, it's hard to stop yourself and you end up getting angry about little things that don't usually bother you. There's been quite a few times that I've snapped at my friends. One time, they were all moaning about their mum or dad and how annoying they are and I got so wound up that I shouted at them to shut up. At least they've got their mum and dad. It sometimes makes me feel so different from them.

It was worse at the start of term. Some friends didn't know what to say or how to act in front of me, so they didn't say anything. I guess they didn't want to upset me but it made me feel really lonely. Luckily one of my close mates, who knew my dad, asked how I was and if I wanted to talk about it. I told him that sometimes I did want to talk about stuff and sometimes I didn't, so they just needed to ask me first. I didn't want them to act all weird, because I like school being normal, but avoiding the subject definitely made it worse.

If I do want to talk about things now I usually talk to Mum or to Will, one of my friends who I play football with. Me and Will weren't that close before, but we started chatting after matches and I found out that his mum died a few years ago. We chat about everything, including my dad and his mum, and he just gets it and knows how I feel. It makes you realize that all your confusing feelings are normal. Talking to Will is what made me agree to go with Mum to a support group in a centre near my house. Luckily there's a really nice counsellor there, so it wasn't too bad. I talk a lot about Dad in the group, which is nice, and I talk to the other kids who have gone through the same. It's good to see that they're still okay and getting on with things. At the moment it still hurts so much that sometimes I can't breathe, but it's good to be reminded that I'll be okay.

TEACHER'S NOTES

Lesson objectives

◇ To encourage children to feel empathy for a peer who has been bereaved and to help them to know what to say and how to act in these circumstances.

Fact file

A school community is likely to be affected by bereavement in some way. This could be the death of a parent as in Niall's story, or a grandparent, friend, teacher or another significant person. Peer support can be extremely useful when a child has experienced a loss but often children do not know how to help or what to say. As in Niall's story, they often end up saying nothing at all, which can lead to the bereaved child feeling isolated and thinking that their friends do not care.

Before delivering lessons on death or bereavement, consider how it will affect any bereaved children in your classroom and if they will need extra support or to sit out of the lesson. It is useful to consult families beforehand to ascertain what the child has been told about the death and what the family's culture is regarding difficult subjects like death, including ethnic and religious beliefs. In some families, the child will have been told age-appropriate details about what has happened, but in others they will not have been told very much at all. Research shows that children are better able to cope with bereavement or serious illness within the family if they are given factual, easy-to-understand, age-appropriate information and are talked to in an open way from the start. Using the words "death" and "died" has been shown to avoid confusion as it helps the child to realize that the person can never come back. Once the child is supported to understand truthful information, they are more able to process what is happening. However, some parents may have tried to protect their children by shying away from the subject or using ambiguous phrases such as "gone to sleep" or "gone to the stars," so consulting them beforehand and respecting their wishes is always advisable.

During lessons about death or bereavement ask the children if they have any questions. If you don't know the answer, it is best to be honest and say you don't know but that you will do your best to help them find the answers. You can explain that no one can know the answers to all the questions they may have about death.

All children react differently to grief and many have conflicting emotions – some might be angry or sad but some might act as if nothing has happened. This does not mean they are not affected by the bereavement – they may not be ready to talk or may want to keep things as normal as possible in school as a break from what is happening at home. Respecting this and monitoring their behaviour is an ongoing process. Unexpressed feelings can sometimes be seen in physical symptoms such as stomach aches or headaches as in Niall's story.

Often children worry that their complex feelings and reactions to grief are not "normal," so they may seek reassurance that whatever they are feeling is a "normal" reaction. The knowledge that many people have felt this way is often helpful. It is always useful to avoid assumptions and to ask the child how they are feeling so that you can be guided by their reactions. Saying you are "sorry for their loss," as Mrs Davies does in the story, rather than avoiding mentioning the subject in case you upset them can help to make the child realize that you care about their welfare and are thinking about them. Teachers are important in modelling the appropriate ways of reacting to and supporting a bereaved person outside the family. The teacher and peers acknowledging what has happened can often help the bereaved child to feel supported. Being there to listen to whatever the child wants to say will also make them feel supported. As is the case for Niall, sometimes the bereaved child may feel unable to talk so openly at home because they are trying to protect their family members. Children also need to know that there is no timescale for the process of grief. You will be there to listen for however long they need.

Some children are not comfortable talking about their feelings, but teachers can also provide activities such as writing, art or role playing, which can help the child to express their feelings in other ways. Some days the child will find it hard to concentrate. Winston's Wish (see the Resources section) has several ideas on how the pupil can communicate to the teacher that they are having a hard day (e.g. time-out cards, giving the pupil permission to leave the class for a break or a worry post box where they can leave messages for the teacher).

Comprehension activities

1. Why is Niall worried about going back to school after the holidays?

2. Why do you think Niall and his mum decide to write a letter for Mrs Davies to read out?

3. Create a Niall's feelings mind map. Draw Niall in the centre of the mind map and show the different feelings that he experiences in the story.

4. Write a list of how Mrs Davies helps to support Niall.

5. Write a letter to Niall asking him how you could help him and telling him you are sorry about his loss.

6. Write a list of suggestions of how you could be a good friend to Niall and support him.

Further activities

1. The teacher should read *Lifetimes* by Bryan Mellonie to the class, which simply explains the cycle of life for humans, plants and animals, and how death is a natural part of that cycle. The teacher should ask the class what they understand by the life cycle. The children should research the life cycle of one of the creatures described in the book and feed back to the rest of the class.

> **Teacher's note** – *Lifetimes* was written in 1983 and states that many people live to be "at least 60 or 70," which may worry some children.

2. Create a poster showing how you could support someone who has suffered a bereavement. Include all the things you could do or say to help. If you have suffered a bereavement you can include things that have helped you.

3. The teacher should ask the students if they have read any books or watched any movies where a character loses someone they loved (e.g. *Up*, *Charlotte's Web*, *Finding Nemo*, *The Lion King*, *Bambi*, *Coco*). The class should discuss how the characters felt and how their behaviour changed when the loved one died.

RESOURCES

Books
Fiction

Durant, A. (2013) *Always and Forever*. London: Picture Corgi.

Ironside, V. (2011) *The Huge Bag of Worries*. London: Hodder Children's Books.

Karst, P. and Lew-Vriethoff, J. (2018) *The Invisible String*. New York: Little, Brown.

Levete, G. (2014) *Talk to My Gran About Dying – My School Project*. London: Third Age Press.

Mellonie, B. and Ingpen, R. ([1983] 2009) *Lifetimes: The Beautiful Way to Explain Death to Children*. London: Bantam Books.

Varley, S. (1984) *Badger's Parting Gifts*. London: Andersen Press.

Non-fiction

Butler, H. (2013) *Helping Children Think about Bereavement*. Abingdon and New York: Routledge.

Chadwick, A. (2011) *Talking about Death and Bereavement in School*. London and Philadelphia, PA: Jessica Kingsley Publishers.

Dyregrov, A. (2008) *Grief in Children: A Handbook for Adults*, 2nd revised edition. London and Philadelphia, PA: Jessica Kingsley Publishers.

Jackson, M. and Colwell, J. (2001) *A Teacher's Handbook of Death*. London and Philadelphia, PA: Jessica Kingsley Publishers.

Jacobs, A. (2013) *Supporting Children through Grief and Loss: Practical Ideas and Creative Activities for Schools and Carers*. Buckingham, UK: Hinton House Publishers.

Jay, C. and Thomas, J. (2012) *What Does Dead Mean?: A Book for Young Children to Help Explain Death and Dying*. London and Philadelphia, PA: Jessica Kingsley Publishers.

Leutner, D. (2009) *Remembering*. London: Child Bereavement Charity.

Pennells, M. and Smith, S. (1999) *Forgotten Mourners: Guidelines for Working with Bereaved Children*, 2nd edition. London and Philadelphia, PA: Jessica Kingsley Publishers.

Romain, T. (2003) *What On Earth Do You Do When Someone Dies?* Minneapolis, MN: Free Spirit Publishing Inc.

Rowling, L. (2003) *Grief in School Communities: Effective Support Strategies*. Philadelphia, PA: Open University Press.

Smith, S.C. (1999) *The Forgotten Mourners: Guidelines for Working with Bereaved Children*, 2nd edition. London and Philadelphia, PA: Jessica Kingsley Publishers.

Stokes, J.A., Crossley, D. and Stubbs, D. (2007) *As Big As It Gets: Supporting a Child When a Parent is Seriously Ill*, 2nd revised edition. London: Winston's Wish.

Ward, B. and associates (1995) *Good grief: Exploring Feelings, Loss and Death with Under 11s*. London and Philadelphia, PA: Jessica Kingsley Publishers.

Whittaker, L. and Mood, P. (2001) *Finding a Way Through When Someone Close Has Died, What It Feels Like and What You Can Do to Help Yourself: A Workbook by Young People for Young People*. London and Philadelphia, PA: Jessica Kingsley Publishers.

Websites

Child Bereavement UK www.childbereavementuk.org

Child Bereavement UK helps children and young people, parents and families to rebuild their lives when a child grieves or when a child dies. It has an excellent dedicated section for schools (early years, primary and secondary) containing a breadth of information, publications, resources and lesson plans. It also has a useful information sheet explaining death to children.

Childhood Bereavement Network www.childhoodbereavementnetwork.org.uk

Childhood Bereavement Network has a link to a directory of childhood bereavement organizations across the UK.

Cruse Bereavement Care www.cruse.org.uk

Cruse Bereavement Care promotes the wellbeing of bereaved people, supporting them to understand their grief and cope with their loss.

Grief Encounter www.griefencounter.org.uk

Grief Encounter supports bereaved children and their families and includes some useful videos.

Hope Again www.hopeagain.org.uk

Hope Again is the interactive youth website of Cruse Bereavement Care, designed for young people by young people. It is a moderated website offering children support after the death of someone close.

Marie Curie www.mariecurie.org.uk

Marie Curie offers useful signposts to support for children and young people who have a close family member who is seriously ill. The organization also produces booklets to support children and young people when someone close has a terminal illness or has died, which can be downloaded from their website.

Winston's Wish www.winstonswish.org

Winston's Wish supports children and young people after the death of a parent or sibling.

4

Oliver Is on the Autism Spectrum

I was already panicking about school on the last day of the summer holidays. I couldn't get rid of the horrible thoughts about my new class. One thought kept turning into another like an avalanche until I had what Mum calls a meltdown, which was really scary. Meltdowns are horrible because you completely lose control of what you're doing and there's nothing you can do about it. I usually cry, scream and shout, and Mum has to try to calm me down. She was trying to get me to breathe deeply and kept saying that school would be fine. She didn't *know* it was going to be fine though, so she shouldn't have said it. And, it turns out, she was wrong. The first day of school was just as hard as last year.

As soon as I put on my new uniform in the morning, I knew I wouldn't be able to concentrate on anything all day. The shirt felt really scratchy like sandpaper. I feel the tiniest of things and then I can't get them out of my head. By the time we got to the school gates, the only thing I could think about was how much my shirt was hurting. Then, everything got worse. All I could hear was loud screeching, which made me want to run away. My heart started beating really fast and it felt like my head was going to explode. I started panicking so much that I wanted to escape from my own body. I'd forgotten how completely terrifying the playground is.

I stood close to Mum and tried to shut everything out. My arms started flapping and I started to hum and tap on my ears to try to block out the noise. It's my way of calming myself down and pushing away panicky feelings and is called stimming. It's really hard to control. It just kind of happens when things get too much or, sometimes, when I'm really happy and excited.

Even though doing all those repetitive actions helps me to calm down, Mum told me that some people stare because they don't understand why I'm doing it. She explained that lots of people have a stim but for them it's usually things like biting their nails or playing with their hair when they're nervous. She said my stims stand out more because they're different so some kids don't understand them. That's probably why it bothers them so much and they keep away from me. I also have other ways of calming myself down like breathing in for five and out for five and tapping my fingers together inside my pockets. Sometimes, that works and I start to feel calm again. But sometimes, like on that first day, everything's too much.

The whole first week of school was horrible, to be honest. Every time the first bell rang I felt sick. It was so loud and I was so nervous about everything – the new kids in the class, the new classroom, the new desks, the new layout, the new teacher. That's a lot of new things. New teachers always make me really jittery because they don't know me and I don't know them. And I'm always terrified of being told off, because sometimes I forget what I should be doing and I find it hard to follow instructions. Sometimes, if a teacher mentions a mistake I've made, it really upsets me and I end up crying. I even panic when teachers shout at the whole class, even if it's nothing to do with me.

Mrs Davies didn't shout too much in the first week but she did keep clapping to get everyone's attention, which made my ears hurt. One thing I did like, though, was that she told us all the rules that we had to follow and they were the same as last year. I was so glad there were no new rules to remember! Rules make me feel safe and make the class go quieter, but it sometimes upsets me if people don't follow them. Like on the second day, when our noise level chart said "whispering voices" and everyone started to chat really loudly. I can't concentrate when it's noisy and sometimes I don't even notice the teacher talking to me, so I started to get angry when the class was ignoring the chart. Mrs Davies did make sure everyone quietened down quite quickly and I think she noticed that I was getting wound up because she came to sit next to me and went over what we were doing. She even wrote it all down for me in a list. That helped because I sometimes can't concentrate on things when she just tells us what to do, especially when it's so noisy.

By half term Mrs Davies knew loads of things that helped me to feel less worried. She let me play with putty in class, which helps me to relax, and reminded me to wear my ear defenders so I could block out the noise. She also let me sit at the end of the row near the door to help me concentrate. It made me more relaxed because I knew I was allowed to leave the room if things got too much. There's this special room I'm allowed to go to if I need to calm down. Mrs Davies uses the number scale, like Mum does, so I can tell her how stressed I am. If I get to a 4, which is really stressed, she sends me for a break. That stops me from getting to a 5!

Mrs Davies also helps when I haven't understood what she's saying. Once we were doing a writing exercise and she said "put your thinking caps on" and then told us all the instructions. But I wasn't able to listen to any of the instructions because I didn't understand what "put your thinking caps on" meant. It made me panic because I didn't know what I was supposed to be doing so I started scribbling on the paper. But she came over and explained it all to me and that calmed me down.

She also started using a picture timetable at the front of the class, which really helped. It meant we could see what was happening that day. The trouble was that once she forgot to change the timetable to tell us that there was a change of plan. The timetable said we should have been doing maths but Mrs Davies said, "Today we're having a special assembly." Special assembly? I didn't know anything about it. I started to panic and I wanted to hide under the table. Everything suddenly felt out of control. I did manage to calm myself down by rocking and tapping my fingers, but then assembly was really bad. The room's massive and echoey and I wanted to run away. I couldn't listen to a word that the head teacher was saying because I was so stressed. As soon as assembly finished, I couldn't get out of there quick enough.

Copyright © Ffion Jones, Helen Cowie and Harriet Tenenbaum – *A School for Everyone* – 2022

Everyone was really excited when we got back to class, but I didn't know why. I found out that the head teacher had said that our class was going to be doing a gardening project. I was so excited because I love gardens. At home, if I need to calm down that's where I go. And because I've helped Mum plant loads of stuff, I know all about flowers and plants.

I made loads of good suggestions in class about what we could plant and everyone seemed to listen to my ideas. That doesn't usually happen, so it was really fun. If I'd get upset during the day Mrs Davies would chat about the garden and telling her all the facts I know about plants helped me to calm down. It made me feel like she was really interested in my ideas too.

Things got a bit easier in class as the year went on because I got to know all the routines and Mrs Davies would remind me if things were going to change. One thing that never gets easier though is the playground. Some kids play chaos tag, which is so confusing. I used to try to join in but I kept getting it wrong so they started leaving me out. I tried playing football instead a few times but I'd get that wrong too. It's like I can't make my body do what I want it to do. The boys started to run away from me but I didn't know why. This year it's worse because it's got way more competitive. They all take it really seriously so don't want me to spoil it. I felt really sad at playtimes but being on my own felt a bit better than all the trouble I caused when I was trying to join in.

Things changed one lunch time though when the Year 6 teacher saw me standing on my own. She said she's started a chess club at lunch breaks and took me over to have a look. I'm really good at playing chess and she even said that we're allowed to eat our lunch when we're playing, so I wouldn't have to go to the noisy canteen anymore. I played a game against Rhys from Year 6 and I won!

I go every lunch time now. In chess club I can outsmart kids much older than me without even talking to them. I know exactly what I'm supposed to be doing there and I'm not worried about what I should say. It's really quiet too, which makes talking to people easier. When me and Rhys are playing we don't really talk much but we sometimes chat afterwards, even if I lose. Sometimes if I lose, I need to calm down on my own but Rhys doesn't mind. He's really kind. That's why I like him. When I don't understand something he's said or I say things wrong or talk too much about the gardening project, he doesn't get cross or ignore me or laugh at me. It doesn't seem to matter to him that I'm different. He's taken time to get to know me and says I'm his most reliable, fair and honest friend. I definitely tell him what I think. He says school would be more boring if I wasn't there!

TEACHER'S NOTES

Lesson objectives

◇ To help pupils understand autism and to encourage them to feel empathy for autistic children with the aim of promoting acceptance of differences.

◇ To celebrate those differences to promote inclusion of everyone in the classroom.

Fact file

Autism is a lifelong condition that affects millions of people. It changes the way the brain works so that autistic people experience the world differently.

Every autistic person is different. Since the autism spectrum affects people in different ways, autistic people may exhibit a wide range of different behaviours. This is why it is called the autism spectrum.

In this story, Oliver struggles with some common difficulties faced by some autistic children. He struggles with communication, a very literal understanding of language, interaction with other children, imaginative play that doesn't follow rules, following instructions, changes to the routine, and he sometimes gets overwhelmed by sensory overload. He has "meltdowns" because he gets overwhelmed but finds it hard to express himself. His repetitive behaviour, or "stimming" (short for self-stimulatory behaviour), such as flapping hands, rocking and humming, helps him to calm down but sometimes children do not accept him because of these behaviours. Autistic children in mainstream schools can be subjected to bullying because other children do not understand the reasons for these behaviours. Making children more autism aware, so that they understand these behaviours, will help to promote peer acceptance.

Some children may not exhibit any of these behaviours at school and appear to be coping (called "masking") when in fact they are extremely stressed. Unstructured times and noisy playgrounds can be particularly difficult. Oliver's story shows how more structured games like chess and board games can be helpful.

In the story the teacher finds some things that help Oliver in the classroom such as writing down instructions simply and clearly to give him more time to process information, using visual supports such as visual timetables, reminding him when a change to the routine is going to happen, incorporating his interest in gardening into the lessons, using a scale that breaks down stress (often called the 5-point scale), and having a designated area where he can calm down and feel safe. The National Autistic Society (see the link in the Resources section) has many practical tips on how teachers can help in an informal way as well as formal strategies that can be used to support autistic children.

Comprehension activities

1. In the story Oliver makes friends with Rhys. Do you think making friends is important to Oliver? Why is making friends important to all of us? Discuss in pairs and feed back to the class.

> **Teacher's note** – Make it clear to the class that children on the autism spectrum often want to make friends like everyone else but sometimes find it hard to interact with others.

2. Write a character profile of Rhys, describing what makes him a good friend to Oliver.

3. List all of the similarities you have with Oliver.

> **Teacher's note** – This encourages students to consider similarities as well as differences.

Further activities

1. Divide your paper into two columns. In pairs, brainstorm what you think autism is. In the left column, write a list of words that come to mind when you think of autism. In the right column, write down a list of things you want to know about autism. Feed back to the rest of the class.

2. Create a spider diagram showing all the things that make you worried or nervous and how you calm yourself down.

> **Teacher's note** – Explain that we all react in various ways to anxieties and we find different ways of coping.

3. Make a list of all the things you find difficult.

> **Teacher's note** – Stress how everyone finds certain things difficult and that we all need help sometimes. You should also point out that everyone finds different things difficult as we are all unique.

4. Look at the common sayings below and then write a sentence explaining them in literal terms.

Raining cats and dogs.
Put your thinking caps on.
Sitting on the fence.
When pigs fly.
You're driving me up the wall.
Let's call it a day.
Keep your eyes peeled.
I'm all ears.
Penny for your thoughts.
Speak of the devil.

> **Teacher's note** – Explain that autistic children often find non-literal language like idioms and metaphors difficult to comprehend. Therefore, it is important to say what you mean or explain the meaning to autistic children.

5. Autistic children sometimes find it difficult to make friends. Think about Oliver's story and create a mind map to show what you could do to make it easier for them in school. Think about how you could include them and make them feel valued.

6. Many famous people are on or are thought to be on the autistic spectrum. Research the following people and find out as much information about them as you can. Create a profile for each one, including all their amazing achievements.

Lewis Carroll
Albert Einstein
Dan Aykroyd
Chris Packham
Temple Grandin

7. Create a poster showing everything you know about autism to raise awareness in the rest of the school. Research the positive features of autism and remember to include these on your poster.

RESOURCES

Books
Fiction

Bailey, J. and Song, M. (2019) *A Friend for Henry*. San Francisco, CA: Chronicle Books.

Baskin, N.R. (2010) *Anything But Typical*, reprint edition. New York and London: Simon & Schuster.

Bishop, B. and Bishop, C. (2011) *My Friend with Autism*, 2nd edition. Sevenoaks, UK: Future Horizons.

Cain, B.S. (2012) *Autism, the Invisible Cord: A Sibling's Diary*, 1st edition. Washington, DC: Magination Press.

Davis, M. (2017) *Superstar*. New York: HarperCollins.

Gaynot, K. (2008) *A Friend Like Simon*, 1st edition. Dublin: Special Stories Publishing.

Scott, L. and Westcott, R. (2019) *Can You See Me?* London: Scholastic.

Non-fiction

Atwood, T. (1998) *Asperger's Syndrome: A Guide for Parents and Professionals*. London and Philadelphia, PA: Jessica Kingsley Publishers.

Brownson, D. (2019) *He's Not Naughty!: A Children's Guide to Autism*. London and Philadelphia, PA: Jessica Kingsley Publishers.

Elder, J. (2005) *Different Like Me: My Book of Autism Heroes*. London and Philadelphia, PA: Jessica Kingsley Publishers.

Faherty, C. (2014) *Autism...What Does It Mean To Me?: A Workbook Explaining Self Awareness and Life Lessons to the Child or Youth With High Functioning Autism or Asperger's*, 2nd edition. Sevenoaks, UK: Future Horizons.

Mosca, J.F. and Rieley, D. (2017) *The Girl Who Thought in Pictures: The Story of Dr. Temple Grandin*. Seattle, WA: The Innovation Press.

Verdick, E. and Reeve, E. (2012) *Survival Guide for Kids with Autism Spectrum Disorders*. Minneapolis, MN: Free Spirit Publishing.

Websites

The Autism Society of America www.autism-society.org

The Autism Society of America has useful general information about autism.

The National Autistic Society www.autism.org.uk

The National Autistic Society website contains resources, practical tips and suggestions to help autistic children in the classroom. It includes information about social stories, created by Carol Gray in 1991, which can be used to help autistic people understand what to do in certain social situations. The website also has links to visual support resources that may be useful.

5

Chris Wants to Be a Girl

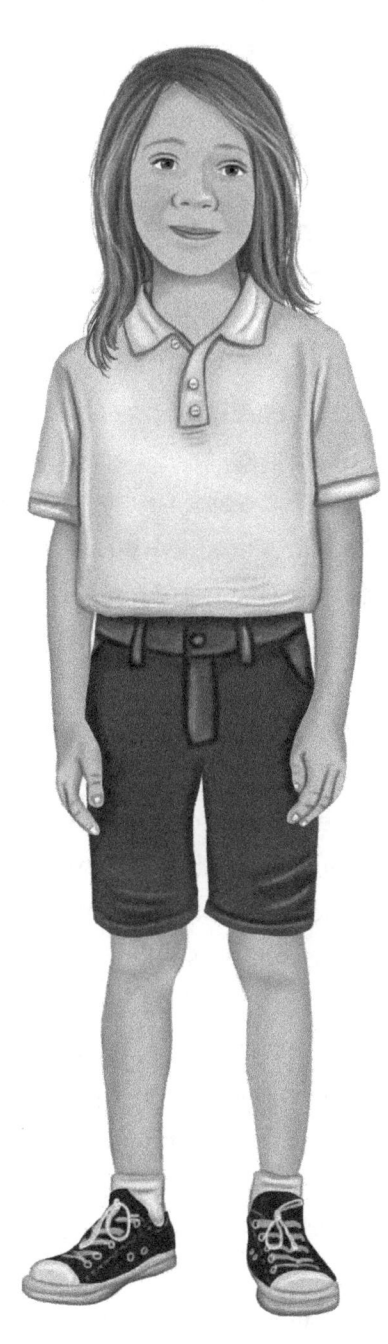

"Children, I would like the girls to line up on this side and boys to line up on this side," said Mrs Davies, as soon as we got to school.

I hate it when we have to get into boys' and girls' lines at school because even though the teacher thinks that I am a boy, I know that I am a girl. I have known I was a girl since I can remember. I always wanted to be a girl. I hate being a boy. It's not my fault I have boy body parts. I was born in the wrong body.

I decided to line up in the boys' line today just so that the other kids wouldn't make fun of me again. Last week, when I got into the girls' line, the other kids laughed at me. One even called me a "weirdo." He said it so quietly that Mrs Davies did not hear him, but loud enough so that all the other kids near us laughed.

At least if I pretend that I am a boy, I can kind of be invisible. I still don't have friends, but at least no one pushes me. Last week, when I lined up on the girls' side, you would not believe what the other kids did. Yasmin told me to "get a haircut" and Niamh just laughed and pulled my hair when Mrs Davies wasn't looking. They sometimes even call me a "he-she."

I figured that today I would get behind Mason and Ollie. They're both really bad at football, even worse than me, so I figured that they would leave me alone. Except that Mason snickered at me and said, "Ha! Now he thinks he's a boy." And Ollie said, "Boys don't have pink water bottles, get in the girl line."

I don't even know why we need to be in lines like this when we're just filling water bottles. And it's so predictable. All the boys had water bottles that were blue or black and mine was pink and purple. These are my favourite colours.

After we got our water, we went back to the class to work with our learning partners. The good thing is that because Mrs Davies thinks I am a boy and she makes all learning partners be opposite genders, I usually work with Becky, which is better than working with one of the boys. I think girls are a bit nicer than boys. And the girls get to do fun stuff like drawing and arts and crafts. The boys just want to do things like play football and rugby and cricket. I hate rugby and football and cricket. It's so boring.

My mum knows I am a girl, but she doesn't know how to help. She worries a lot about me. She even brought me to the doctor. The doctor asked me lots of questions and said that she would make an appointment for me to talk some more with someone else in London, but that was over a year ago. That was after I wore a pink vest to school under my polo shirt. I didn't know we would have PE that day. Just my luck. We needed to change into our PE kits and Dean saw me changing into my PE top. He started telling everyone, "Look, the weirdo is wearing pink! Boys don't wear pink." I said I wasn't a boy. He kept repeating what he was saying. He didn't even listen to me.

Mrs Davies overheard. She told Dean to go to the office. She didn't say anything to me. That night, I heard my parents arguing.

"It's your fault for indulging this silliness," I heard my dad tell my mother.

"But it's not Chris's fault. I've been reading so much stuff about this. Could you please read something about this rather than blaming me?!" I heard my mum argue back.

They kept arguing so I put a pillow over my head and cried all night.

I didn't know what "indulging" meant so I asked my mum the next day. She asked me where I heard that word. I told her that I heard her and Dad arguing. She told me that no matter what, she loved me and so did my dad. She said he would get used to it. It took a long time, but she was right. My dad stopped trying to make me play football with him. He lets me watch *Dancing with Skates* now. And when no one is coming over, he lets me wear the dresses that my mum bought. He said that he thinks I will change my mind soon. I don't think I will. I want to be a girl.

TEACHER'S NOTES

Lesson objectives

◇ To understand difficulties faced by children with gender dysphoria. Gender dysphoria is being unhappy with one's assigned sex at birth.

Fact file

About 50 children per week are referred to clinics in the UK for gender dysphoria. About a quarter of those referred will continue to feel gender dysphoria into adulthood. Those who report gender dysphoria after puberty are more likely to continue to have gender dysphoria into adulthood. Children who are diagnosed with gender dysphoria may be given puberty blockers. Surgery is not performed on people younger than 18 years of age.

Help and support for children and young people who are transgender

There has been a rapid increase in children with gender dysphoria in the UK. The Tavistock remains the only NHS clinic in the UK that can help children, so the waiting list is long. There are things teachers and schools can do in the meantime to make the environment more welcoming for trans children, such as encourage the wearing of gender-neutral uniforms and shoes, make sure that toilets are gender neutral and not organize the classroom based on sex. In this story, the teacher often uses gender as a way to organize the classroom. For example, she has children line up based on gender and pairs children so that boys and girls work together. By doing so, she organizes the classroom based on gender, which makes gender more obvious. Research indicates that organizing a classroom based on gender leads to lower opinions of the other gender and more traditional gender attitudes in children. It also excludes children who do not categorize themselves into one of the genders, such as children with gender dysphoria or children with an intersex condition (about 1% of people have anatomy that differs from what is typical for their biological sex).

Comprehension activities

1. Explain to children what gender dysphoria (being unhappy with one's assigned sex at birth) and cisgender (being content with one's assigned sex at birth) are.

CHRIS WANTS TO BE A GIRL

2. In the story, the teacher has the children line up by gender. How does this make Chris feel? Do you think that this practice is fair for all children?

3. How else could the teacher ask the children to line up? For example:

   What if the teacher asked children to line up by month of birthday?

   What if the teacher asked children to line up by eye colour?

Further activities

1. In pairs, write a letter to Mrs Davies explaining how lining up by gender makes some children feel.

2. Think about ways you are similar and different to your classmates. Draw a picture of yourself and write down the ways you are different from your classmates that make you happy.

RESOURCES

Gender Equality Matters www.genderequalitymatters.eu/consortium

> Gender Equality Matters is a consortium that promotes equality for lesbian, gay, bisexual, trans and intersex individuals. They have useful YouTube videos with songs for children: www.genderequalitymatters.eu/toolkits/multimedia-resources

Mermaids https://mermaidsuk.org.uk

> Mermaids is a charity that works with gender-diverse children.

School Wellbeing www.schoolwellbeing.co.uk/uploads/chronicler/document/document/1018/R0566_Trans_Inclusion_Toolkit_for_Schools.pdf

> School Wellbeing, the health and wellbeing service organized by Leeds City Council, has a toolkit with lesson plans.

The Tavistock https://tavistockandportman.nhs.uk/about-us/kids-edge-channel-4-documentary/kids-edge-gender-clinic

> The Tavistock is the NHS gender clinic for all children in the UK. Its website has valuable resources including a documentary.

The Times Higher Education Supplement www.tes.com/articles/transgender-teaching-resources

> *The Times Higher Education Supplement* has resources and lesson plans for teaching about transgender issues.

Welcoming Schools www.welcomingschools.org/resources/definitions/youth-definitions

> Welcoming Schools has a list of ways of defining terms for young children.

6

Michael Learns About Important Black Britons

My name is Michael. I live with my mum, dad and little sister, Kimona.

I like school and have lots of friends. I do well in school. Mum makes me do all the assignments plus the extensions on every assignment. Not only that, but she pays for a tutor for me so that I can be a year ahead in maths. She says that we need to work twice as hard as white people to get to the same place. She is always being turned down for promotions at work, but she works very hard. She's a nurse at the hospital in town. I know she loves me, but it's so annoying that she makes me do every bit of every assignment when I know no one else in school always has to do them. School is easy anyway, but I don't always put my hand up for every question because I don't want the other kids to think I'm a swot. Also, we're always doing work that is too easy.

For a bit, my dad couldn't find a job. Mum thought maybe it was because his name was D'andre Johnson so it sounded like he was not British even though he was born here. His middle name is Clive so he started sending out job applications with his name as D. Clive Johnson. Now, he's found a job.

I also don't like that we always learn about white people in history. I know that Mary Seacole was a nurse like my mum. But other people in my class don't know any of this. That was until last week. Last week, that all changed, when Mrs Davies told us we would learn about Black history. Turned out it was even better than that. It wasn't just our class. It was a whole-school theme. And it wasn't just history.

When we got to assembly that day, we learnt about famous Black writers. We learnt about Chimamanda Ngozi Adichie, who is a writer from Nigeria. And Zadie Smith, Andrea Levy, Lemn Sissay and Benjamin Zephaniah. Our head teacher even read us some poems that Benjamin Zephaniah wrote! I just had no idea that there were so many. We also watched a TED talk by Chimamanda Ngozi Adichie. We had a long conversation in assembly about what a stereotype is – how when we only know one thing about someone or a group, we think that this is the whole story.

When we got to class, Mrs Davies said we would learn about a famous Black Briton each day. On Monday, we learnt about Mary Seacole and how she was a nurse who helped lots of people. On Tuesday, we learnt about Samuel Coleridge-Taylor, a famous composer. I had no idea that there were so many famous Black Britons in history. On Wednesday, we learnt about a current MP named David Lammy. It's the first time I realized that maybe I could be an MP.

I actually started to really look forward to going to school to learn even more. And it was great to learn about all the different things people did.

TEACHER'S NOTES

Lesson objectives

◇ To help reduce racism in the classroom and to instil pride in African and Caribbean British children.

◇ To give children and teachers an opportunity to discuss race and related issues.

Fact file

The Institute for Race Relations (www.irr.org.uk) in the UK has information about the struggle for racial justice in the UK. Over 87 per cent of the UK is white (see www.irr.org.uk/research/statistics/ethnicity-and-religion/#:~:text=The%20 most%20recent%20Census%20in,other%20groups%200.6%20per%20cent). Children from BAME (Black and minority ethnic) backgrounds are more likely to qualify for free school meals than are white children. Black people are 28 times more likely to be stopped and searched than are white people in the UK.

Help and support for children and young people
Children's books

Calno, M., Collins, M. and Hazzard, A. (2018) *Something Happened in Our Town: A Child's Story about Racial Injustice*. Washington, DC: American Psychological Association.

The book takes place after a police shooting of an African-American man. You can find an interview with the authors here: www.apa.org/pubs/magination/441B228

www.huffingtonpost.co.uk/entry/21-childrens-books-every-black-kid-should-read_n_565 f176be4b072e9d1c43b0a

The weblink above has a list of 21 children's books every Black child should read. Some, such as *Tar Beach* by Faith Ringgold, have won the prestigious Caldecott award. There is even a link to the author reading her story here: www.youtube.com/watch?v=h9RKJleFdBU

Hoffman, M. (1991) *Amazing Grace*. London: Frances Lincoln Children's Books.

Amazing Grace is a classic that shows children that there are no limits to what they can achieve.

O, The Oprah Magazine www.oprahmag.com/entertainment/a32802783/childrens-books-racism

The weblink above gives a list of essential books for discussing racism with children. Many of these books are from the US because fewer than 4 per cent of children's books in the UK have BAME characters (see https://clpe.org.uk).

Benjamin Zephaniah, who is one of the greatest post-war British writers and has seven honorary doctorates, is a Black Briton who has written excellent books of poetry.

Some recommendations are *Wicked World!* and *Funky Chicken*. His autobiography for children is titled, *My Story*. His website may be found here: https://benjaminzephaniah.com

Brown, E. (1994) *Handa's Surprise*. London: Mantra Publishing Ltd.

Handa's Surprise is a book that focuses on a Kenyan girl. The author and illustrator of this book, Eileen Brown, explains why diversity in main characters is so important in this interview: www.booktrust.org.uk/news-and-features/features/2019/september/twenty-five-years-since-handas-surprise-heres-why-eileen-browne-thinks-her-picture-book-has-been-so-loved

Comprehension activities

In pairs, discuss the following:

1. Can you think of an example of something that is unfair in the story?

2. How does the example of Michael's dad not getting a job or his mum not being promoted make him feel? In what ways are these examples of racism?

3. What made Michael excited to go to school?

Further activities

1. In this TED talk (www.ted.com/talks/chimamanda_ngozi_adichie_the_danger_of_a_single_story?language=en), Chimamanda Ngozi Adichie discusses the danger of a single story and how it is important not to think that any one person or group only has one.

   One idea would be to show the talk in class and then lead a discussion about how we all have stereotypes and what we can do about them.

2. Celebrating difference (www.commonsensemedia.org/blog/that-time-i-found-media-to-help-my-kid-embrace-his-hair-and-teach-his-preschool-class-to).

   Have the children create a poster about themselves. In this poster, they should draw a picture of themselves. Below the poster, they could list one thing that makes them unique and another thing that they share with other members of the class.

3. Have children define what racism and discrimination are.

   They could write about how racism and discrimination may affect how other people view people of colour. They could give a specific example of racism (e.g. not including someone in play because of the colour of their skin).

4. In pairs, children could design a poster presentation about one Black Briton.

They could share what they learn with the class. To get you started, here is a link to a few well-known Black Britons: www.theguardian.com/world/2020/jun/12/which-black-britons-should-we-be-commemorating-william-cuffay-mary-seacole

5. Although the following lessons are aimed at children in Key Stages 3 and 4, there are good resources that could be adapted for children who are younger. For example, there is a photograph of a man protesting in a pub that did not allow Black people inside in the early 1960s. Racial discrimination was not illegal in the UK until 1965 (http://s3-eu-west-2.amazonaws.com/wpmedia.outlandish.com/irr/2017/11/17142427/Racial_Discrimination.pdf).

To adapt this lesson for younger children, children could discuss how they would feel if they were not allowed to enter a restaurant. They could write a letter to the owner explaining why they felt the way that they did and what the proprietor could do to remedy the situation.

RESOURCES

www.pbs.org/newshour/nation/making-people-aware-of-their-implicit-biases-doesnt-usually-change-minds-but-heres-what-does-work?fbclid=IwAR2XavenOieFS9Gc_nDN7PrN9vC_XXxd9gnUuo5gUs4lwrOTokR28DpWJUc

This section is for teachers to learn more. There has recently been a lot of focus on unconscious bias. The weblink above leads to an interview with Dr Anthony Greenwald discussing what works and what does not work to reduce prejudice.

SPRING TERM

7

Jamie's Secret

His Dad Is in Prison

Me and my dad have – or rather used to have – a great time together. He taught me how to play football and we used to go every Saturday to this club where we played in different teams all morning. Afterwards we would go to a café and have fish and chips. I was always starving after football! On the way home we would sing songs together in the car. I loved being with my dad.

But all that changed early one morning. The doorbell rang just as it was getting light and suddenly police came barging into my house with dogs. They even came into my bedroom and told me to get out of bed while they searched for something. Then through the bedroom window I saw them take my dad away in handcuffs. Then Mum came into my bedroom and said that I had to go to school as usual. She wouldn't say anything more. I felt sick and confused. What had happened? Was my dad a criminal? That wasn't possible. All day long I felt as if I was frozen. I hardly heard anything the teacher said and stayed by myself at break time and lunch time. When I got home, Mum told me that Dad had been arrested and wouldn't be coming back for a while.

My first question was, "Is Dad a criminal?"

Mum said, "No. He just got in with a bad crowd and he was the one who got caught. We mustn't talk about them or we will be in trouble too."

My next question was, "What about football on Saturday?"

She really bit my head off then. "Football!! Well, you're not going and that's that. Football is the least of my worries!!"

I couldn't speak. I felt so angry with Mum and I ran up to my bedroom and cried and cried for hours. Later Mum came up and explained that what had happened to Dad was a secret and we mustn't talk about it with anyone.

That was very hard. It made me feel apart from the people I had been friends with before. I felt sad all the time and spent more and more time on my own. Sometimes it felt as if the secret inside me would explode. No one ever asked me about Dad but some kids asked why I had stopped going to the club. I told them that I don't want to play football anymore. They looked a bit surprised.

One day, I was thinking about my dad and remembering the days when we had fun together. I didn't notice that Mrs Davies was asking people to get into pairs for football practice. The only person left to choose was William. Of course, no-one had chosen him as he's absolutely rubbish at football because he's so clumsy. My heart sank. But after a moment I asked him if he would like to practise some moves and he said yes.

In the end, I enjoyed it a lot as I had so much to teach him, just as my dad had taught me. I said to him, "Why don't we do this again? You could be quite good with a bit of practice," and he went all red and smiled at me for the first time.

After that, we sometimes played football together, except when he was with his friends, Dean and Liam. I never play with them as they're so scary.

One day, William said that he had a secret to tell me. A secret!! My heart started to beat hard. He told me that he was very worried because Dean and Liam wanted him to go shoplifting with them and he didn't want to. He said, "I don't want to get into trouble but they keep asking me and they laugh at me when I say no. They are my best friends so it's hard."

I found myself blurting out, "You don't want to get into a bad crowd like that. Then you might really become a criminal." And suddenly I found myself telling him about Dad and how he had bad friends who got him into such trouble that he is now in prison. William looked serious then. I thought he was going to cry. I said to him, "Please don't be upset but promise not to tell anyone my secret and I won't tell yours." He smiled at me then and I smiled back. For me it was such a relief to have told my secret to someone.

WILLIAM: GIVING AWAY SOMEONE'S SECRET

I've been worried for days because my friends Liam and Dean want me to go shoplifting with them. I know it's wrong and I just don't want to but they won't be friends with me if I say "No." Last week I was paired up with Jamie, who is the best in the class at football. Usually he ignores me but this time he was friendly and really kind to me. He taught me some skills. Since then, we've played a few times and it's always fun. Because he's so kind, I told him about what's happening with Dean and Liam. He really understood and told me a very big secret, which I promised never to tell anyone. So, when Dean asked me again to go shoplifting with him and Liam, I felt strong enough to say that it was wrong and I would not do it.

Dean laughed at me. "Who says it's wrong?" and I replied, "Jamie does – and he should know!!"

Dean said, "What does he know? He's never short of anything and he gets all that posh football kit for nothing."

Before I could stop myself, I said, "Well he does know 'cos his dad…" And then I stopped and felt myself go all hot and red.

"What about his dad?" shouted Dean. "Come on, Liam. Let's get it out of him!!" And they started punching me until it hurt.

In the end I told them about Jamie's dad and they stopped punching me, but they laughed in a horrible way.

Next day everyone started to talk about Jamie's secret. Dean and Liam had spread it all over Snapchat so everyone knew. I felt sick. Jamie had been so nice to me and look what I had done. I think he was very ashamed because for two days after that he didn't come to school. Not only that, Liam and Dean had used my phone to spread the rumour about Jamie's dad so everyone thought I was a complete snitch. And Dean and Liam have stopped playing with me so now I have no friends left. I am sure that Jamie will never speak to me again.

JAMIE: WHAT DO YOU DO WHEN THE SECRET IS OUT?

Luckily for me Mrs Davies rang my mum to ask how I was. She told her that someone (she mentioned no names) had spread a rumour that my dad was in prison. My mum then told her the truth and Mrs Davies said that there is plenty of help out there for families like ours and that she could set things up. Next day I went back to school and Mrs Davies told me to wait in class at break time. She said she knew about a project worker who could help families where the dad was in prison. I met with him a few days later. He is called Steve and he has been amazing. He helped me understand why I had been feeling so sad and he even found a football club near to school where he could take me on Saturday mornings. He arranged for me to write to Dad and go to see him. That was difficult but Dad told me how much he missed me and that meant a lot to me.

Mrs Davies also got me, William, Dean and Liam together to talk things through. She said what they did was called cyberbullying. It turned out that William had told my secret because Dean and Liam were bullying him and that he had nothing to do with putting it on Snapchat. I still avoid Dean and Liam as they didn't seem at all bothered by what they had done, but William is different. He was very sorry. I could see that from the way he looked at me. So now we are still friends and, you know, he looks a bit fitter after playing football with me. That pleased me a lot!

TEACHER'S NOTES

Lesson objectives

- ◇ To introduce pupils to the issue of children who have a relative in prison and to help them feel some empathy for what that must be like for a child.

Fact file

Over 200,000 children a year in the UK see a parent go to prison. Mostly it is their dads that they see go. There are no statistics on how many children see a brother or sister, grandparent or other close family member go to prison, but that will affect thousands more children each year. In many cases, children are living in what seems like a normal loving family home and then, suddenly, one day, someone close to them vanishes and they can see that the people around them are stressed and unhappy. Then they know that there is some kind of secret but no one is telling them what is going on. So, they feel worried, sad, upset and scared. Often, they are told lies or half truths about why the family member is no longer there. They may even wonder if somehow it is their fault.

Spurgeons (see www.spurgeons.org) provides disturbing statistics about the outcomes for the children of prisoners and the risks that they run:

- ◇ 65 per cent of boys with a convicted parent go on to offend.

- ◇ 37 per cent of prisoners have a family member convicted of a crime.

- ◇ 29 per cent of prisoners experienced abuse as a child.

- ◇ 63 per cent of prisoners had been excluded or temporarily suspended from school.

Help and support for children and young people

There are charities that provide important services for the children in this situation. For example, Barnardo's has partnered with Her Majesty's Prison and Probation Service to provide information and training for professionals as well as practical support and guidance for the children directly affected. They have project workers who will go into school or the home to talk to children and help them to cope with this difficult situation in their lives.

In the story, Jamie was devastated by the experience of seeing his dad being taken away in handcuffs by the police. He also found it hard to deal with the fact that his family wanted the situation to be kept secret. So, all his unhappiness had to be kept bottled up inside him leaving him confused, angry and hurt. He missed his dad very much but, like many other children whose parent is in prison, was not initially allowed to visit his dad, so adding to the mystery surrounding the crime and the sentence. When he did finally tell his secret to William, his friendship was betrayed when William was forced to tell the secret and was cast as the cyberbully who had spread the rumour on Snapchat.

Fortunately, in this case, the class teacher had knowledge of the practical help available for children of prisoners and she was able to link Jamie up with Steve, a project worker from Barnardo's, who helped Jamie regain his confidence and belief in himself and facilitated some visits to the prison. The secret was out but Mrs Davies' action challenged the cyberbullying aspect of the rumour-spreading so a reconciliation took place between Jamie and William.

Comprehension activities

1. How did Jamie feel when his dad was taken away in handcuffs?

2. Why do you think that his mum wanted to keep it a secret?

3. Why were Dean and Liam so pleased to hear that Jamie's dad was in prison?

Further activities

1. Is it a good idea to share secrets with your best friends?

2. Working in small groups, on a large piece of paper, list all the qualities of a good friend. Each group should put their list up on the wall and present their list of qualities to the whole class.

3. Thinking about Liam, Dean and William, discuss whether they really are good friends with one another. List the ways in which they are unkind to one another. Why does William call Liam and Dean his best friends?

4. If someone in your class is having a difficult time, as Jamie was, how can you help to make them feel better? Each group prepares a role play in which a child who is unhappy about a family situation is helped by his classmates. As an introduction to this activity, the teacher can show one of the case studies from the PACT (Prisoners Families Communities: A Fresh Start Together) website (www.prisonadvice.org.uk).

5. Think of a Secret. This is an activity that is suitable for children in Years 5 and 6 rather than younger age groups. The class sits in a circle. Each child is asked to think about a secret thing that they have never told anyone about. This could be a secret fear, an everyday concern, a hope for the

future, a dream about what they would like to become, something they wish they hadn't done or just something that nobody knows about them. **IT IS IMPORTANT TO STRESS THAT THEY ARE NOT ASKED TO SAY WHAT THAT SECRET IS.** The children look around the circle and think of someone who they might be able to tell their secret to. **AGAIN, STRESS THAT THEY WILL NOT BE ASKED TO IDENTIFY THIS PERSON OR SHARE THE SECRET WITH THEM.** Next, on a card they write down the qualities of that person that make them think that they could share their secret with them. Finally, the whole class puts their cards in the middle of the circle and the teacher writes the qualities up on a large sheet of paper. The whole group then discusses what are the good things about these qualities. Prompt questions could include:

How hard is it to share a secret?

How many of you identified with the qualities that went up on the large sheet of paper?

How difficult is it to keep a secret?

How did you react when someone told you a secret in the past?

The teacher ends the discussion by making the point that all the qualities listed on the large sheet of paper are present within this class. "We have all these qualities among us. Let's try to build on them!!"

RESOURCES

Barnardo's www.barnardos.org.uk

> Barnardo's has a useful section on its website about the families of prisoners. It has also partnered with Her Majesty's Prison and Probation Service to create the National Information Centre on Children of Offenders (NICCO) (www.nicco.org.uk), which provides training for all professionals who come into contact with the children and families of offenders as well as services to support children and their families affected by a parent in prison. It has project workers who will go into school or the home to talk to children and help them to cope with this difficult situation in their lives.

Childline www.childline.org.uk

> Childline has a useful section on its website for the children of incarcerated parents. It provides resources and support services as well as illustrative case studies on the emotions experienced by children in this situation. Childline also emphasizes the child's right to feel safe at home and offers the opportunity for children to talk in confidence about their issues.

Pact (Prisoners Families Communities: A Fresh Start Together) www.prisonadvice.org.uk

Helpline for prisoners' families: 0808 808 2003

> Pact is a national charity that helps prisoners, people with convictions and their families to make a fresh start. Its aim is to minimize the harm that can be caused by imprisonment. Its vision is of a society where justice is understood as a process of restoration and healing in which prisons are used sparingly and as places of learning and rehabilitation. Pact has a long-standing concern for the families of prisoners, providing services for children and young people involved. Pact has a special section on its website for children and for the professionals around them, containing moving testimonies in the words of the children themselves. Pact also provides a helpline as a safe space where children can talk about what they feel and what their worries are about their parent in prison.

Prison Fellowship www.prisonfellowship.org

> Prison Fellowship, based in the US, is a Christian charity that serves prisoners, former prisoners and their families, and is a leading advocate for prison reform. This organization provides volunteers to give respite to caregivers and support to children through such activities as summer camps and local sports centres. Its aim is to work collaboratively for justice that is restorative rather than punitive.

Spurgeons www.spurgeons.org

> This organization aims to improve the lives of children and their families who are affected by a parent being in prison. Its website has moving testimonies from children about what it is like to have a parent in prison. Spurgeons supports children's visits to their parent; it also provides a mentoring and support service for children and young people. Spurgeons aims to break the cycle of criminal activity that could lead to reoffending.

8

Kerry and the Food Bank

I don't usually talk to other people about my family having no money because I feel ashamed. Often it makes me very sad to think about it. It makes me feel different from my friends, so I often spend more and more time on my own. There are so many things I just can't do any more, like going on school trips, buying new things at the shops or having an ice cream in the café or buying my friends presents for their birthday. Some children laugh at you if your clothes are old and sometimes a bit crumpled and dirty. Sometimes I'm so angry about having no money that I could explode.

Me, Mum and my little brother Danny used to have a nice flat, but after Dad left, Mum couldn't pay the rent so we had to move. The first place was horrible. It was called Woodland House, but there were no woods that I could see and the view from the window was of an ugly lorry park. There were no shops or cafés or anywhere for children to play as the council had converted all the flats from a huge, out-of-town office block. Woodland House was miles from anywhere and we had such a long walk to the bus stop to get to school each morning. It was so cold in the winter that we had to spend a lot of time wrapped in blankets just to keep warm. And it was small. We didn't even have room for a table, so all our stuff was stacked on the floor in plastic bags. It was noisy too with people shouting and fighting right outside our door some nights. At least it was temporary, so after a few months we were rehoused in a proper flat which is much nicer and it is closer to school. But my mum still has hardly any money.

One afternoon after school Mum counted out all the money she had that day and told us there was just enough for some chips. When we arrived at the chippy, Mum said, "A large bag of chips please."

The man behind the counter said, "Do you want any fish then?"

Mum said, "No thanks. We're fine with chips."

But the man saw my look as I eyed the tasty fish in batter ready to be dropped into the fat. My mouth was watering at the sight of it. I couldn't believe it when he just popped a big fried fish into the bag of chips and handed it to my mum, who hadn't noticed. He gave me a big wink. When we got home, Mum was amazed, but I didn't tell her that maybe I had something to do with it. Anyway, we sat around with the fish and large helpings of chips and it was like a feast. Mum laughed for once and we all sat together eating and chatting. It was just like how we used to be before Mum stopped having any money.

But other nights weren't so good and we went to bed hungry. Our school has a breakfast club, so one morning I had big helpings of cereal and toast as I was starving!! Mrs Davies noticed that I was having second helpings of everything and she asked me if I was all right. As she is such a kind teacher, I decided to tell her the reason – that none of my family had any dinner the night before or the night before that – so my little brother and I were hungry. She looked very upset when she heard this. Later in the day, she said that she had written a letter to my mum telling her about the food bank. I didn't know what a food bank was but thought that it sounded very exciting if it gave out food like a cashpoint at the bank.

When Mum read the letter, at first she was very angry, and started muttering things like "We don't need any charity, thank you very much," but after a while she said that we would give it a try. So, the next day, after school, we set off for the food bank. It was three miles from our flat! Walking there was fun as the sun was shining and we were so happy at the thought of having some food in the house. Walking back was a different story. Even though Mum carried the heaviest bags, Danny and I had to carry two bags each.

When it started to rain, Danny kept whining, "Mum, can't we get the bus?"

And she snapped back, "If we could afford the bus fare we wouldn't be going to the food bank, would we?"

So that was that.

The next time we went to the food bank I met a girl from my class, so I realized that we are not the only family with problems. We have been able to talk about it a bit and it is great to be with someone who really knows what it is like to have no money. The food bank has a café with a play area, so we have enjoyed being with each other there. It is lovely and warm, and the helpers are very friendly.

Now that we are living nearer to the centre of town it will be easier for Mum to find a job. Soon she is going to work as an office cleaner two evenings a week so perhaps things will get better for us. That's my dream!!

TEACHER'S NOTES

Lesson objectives

◇ To introduce pupils to the issue of children who live in poverty and to help them feel some empathy for what that must be like for a child.

Fact file

One-fifth of UK families live in poverty. The UK government's most recent poverty figures show that more than 4 million children are growing up in poverty, a rise of 500,000 over five years. The outcomes for children living in poverty are serious, with a high risk of poorer mental health, wellbeing and physical health, underachievement at school, and experience of bullying and stigma at school. Two-thirds of children living in poverty are in working families.

Austerity measures affecting families have had a particularly detrimental impact on the children. For example, parents on zero-hours contracts, people in the gig economy and people working in two or three different jobs are often not able to earn enough money to look after their children in the ways that they would like. Schools often provide clothes and food for children so that they can get through the day.

Help and support for children and young people

A range of organizations provide important services for children living in poverty. For example, the Joseph Rowntree Foundation (JRF) provides up-to-date information. JRF funds research projects to document the extent of child poverty in the UK and makes strong, evidence-based policy recommendations to the government. The Trussell Trust supports a nationwide network of food banks that provide emergency food and support to individuals and families locked in poverty. The Trust also campaigns for change to end the need for food banks in the UK. Between April 2018 and March 2019, the Trussell Trust distributed a record 1.6 million food bank parcels. The Children's Society campaigns to ensure that every local council adequately funds emergency support for families desperate for support at a time of crisis. Schools and churches also play an important role in helping families living in poverty through provision of breakfast clubs and school lunches.

In the story, Kerry was very upset by the change in her family's circumstances after they had to leave their home because her mother could not pay the rent. Encouraged by the kindness of the man behind the counter in the chip shop, she confided in her teacher, who was able to put the family in touch with the local food bank. There, the volunteers would provide not only food but also advice and information to Kerry's mum. Meanwhile, the school was able to provide Kerry and her brother with breakfast and free lunches.

Comprehension activities

1. How did Kerry feel when her mum said that they had little money for food?

2. What did Kerry think of Woodland House?

3. Why do you think that her mum did not want to go to the food bank at first?

4. What steps did Kerry take to ensure that the family had enough to eat?

Further activities

1. There are some case studies on the Trussell Trust website, e.g. *Sarah's Story* and *Marcella's Story* (www.trusselltrust.org), which show what a food bank is like. Working in small groups, brainstorm ways to make the food bank more welcoming and friendly for children.

2. Kerry hated living in Woodland House. Working in pairs or small groups, on a large piece of paper, plan a design to make Woodland House more suitable for families to live in. Think about the inside of the flats (heating, cooking, bathrooms, storage) as well as the environment outside (gardens, play areas, transport facilities). Once the task is finished, each group should put their design up on the wall and present their plans to the whole class.

RESOURCES

Books and articles

Hudson, K. (2019) *Lowborn*. London: Chatto & Windus.

> In this book, Kerry Hudson vividly describes what it is like to live in poverty as she revisits, as an adult, the places where she grew up. As a child, she was constantly on the move with her single mother, living in bed and breakfast accommodation and council flats, and consequently attending nine primary schools and five secondary schools.

Rhodes, E. (2019) "From poverty to flourishing." *The Psychologist, December*, 10–11.

Websites

Joseph Rowntree Foundation www.jrf.org.uk

> Joseph Rowntree Foundation's (2016) publication "Growing up in poverty detrimental to children's friendships and family life" (www.jrf.org.uk/press/growing-poverty-detrimental-children's-friendships-and-family-life) proposes that children who experience poverty are more likely to have problems with relationships, including an increased likelihood of being bullied and fighting with their friends, and having less communicative relationships with friends and family. These problems have an impact on how well children perform at school and their likelihood of finding a way out of poverty as adults.

> JRF also found that children who have experienced poverty, particularly persistent poverty, are:

> More likely to be solitary. More than a third of children in persistent poverty were described as tending to play alone, compared to a quarter of children who have never experienced poverty.

> Three times as likely to fall out with their friends "most days" (9% of children in persistent poverty compared to 3% of those who had never experienced poverty).

> Four times more likely to fight with or bully other children (16% of those in persistent poverty, compared to 4% of those who had never been poor). They are also more than twice as likely to report being bullied frequently themselves (12% compared to 5% of the never poor).

> Less likely to talk to their friends about their worries (34% of those in persistent poverty, compared to 43% of the never poor).

> More likely to spend time with their friends outside school. Half of children (50%) in persistent poverty say they see their friends outside school most days, compared with a third (35%) of children who had never been in poverty.

The Children's Society www.childrenssociety.org.uk

> This charity aims to fight child poverty and neglect and help all children have a better chance in life. According to their definition, a child is said to be living in poverty when they are living in a family with an income below 60 per cent of the UK's average after adjusting for family size. Almost two-thirds of children living in poverty have at least one parent in work. This shows that, for many, work simply isn't paying enough for parents to provide for their children. As they indicate, parents living in poverty are skipping meals

so they can afford to feed their children, and in winter many families are forced to make the impossible choice between feeding their children or heating their homes. Low wages make it difficult for families to escape poverty and it is even harder when at the same time the prices of everyday essentials like food and fuel are rising.

The Trussell Trust www.trusselltrust.org

The Trussell Trust aims to end hunger and poverty in the UK. Its annual report paints a stark picture of what poverty means for daily life. People on low incomes spend more of their income compared to the average on essentials – food, utilities, rent, bus fares and so on. When they are swept into deeper poverty, they are often forced to cut back the food budget. Many of these families also go without other essentials and are excluded from opportunities to learn, to enjoy life and to improve their prospects. To release children and families from this situation, the Trussell Trust argues that we need to redesign the systems that trap them there, such as housing and labour markets and social security systems. The report indicates key successful steps to begin this process.

9

Harrison, Sophie and Aria Worry About Body Image

HARRISON

"Please remember your kits on Thursday because we're playing netball!" Mrs Davies said cheerfully, as if everyone would be really excited. I, for one, wasn't. As soon as she mentioned netball, I was dreading it.

I used to look forward to PE lessons, whatever game we were playing, but that changed last term when our class played netball for the first time. Everyone was lined up, waiting to be chosen by Dean and Niamh, the team captains. I had a feeling I wouldn't get picked first, because I'm the shortest in the class and I knew they'd think that being tall would help to score goals! But I didn't expect to be picked last – I'm one of the sportiest in the class. Being picked last wasn't the worse thing though. As I was standing there, with a few others who are usually left at the end, some of the class started giggling. And they were looking right at me.

"Dean said he wasn't picking Titch because he's too short to score!" I heard one giggling.

No one had ever called me "Titch" before. No one had even pointed out how short I was until then because it wasn't really an issue. I mean, I know I'm short but it hadn't bothered me, or anyone else, up until that point.

All through the match everyone kept calling out "Titch" when they wanted me to pass to them. And then I started playing really badly because I felt really self-conscious and embarrassed. After the match, the "Titch" nickname just stuck. Even my friends started calling me it. I laughed it off and pretended I didn't care but I hated it and started hating netball too because that's when it all started.

Thursday's PE lesson came too quickly and I was in a bad mood all morning.

"What's up?" my friend Mason asked.

I grunted and said I hated netball.

"I wish I was as good as you at sports," he said.

Mason is really clumsy but always tries his best. He's always picked last but he doesn't seem to mind – sports just isn't his "thing." He's into American comics and he's brilliant at drama. I thought about what he said and realized he was right: I was usually quite good at sports. I'm really fast and can dart quickly between people. I started to feel a bit silly that I'd let some lame nickname put me off while Mason always gets on with it, usually with a big smile on his face. It wasn't like me to let people's opinions change the way I act.

"Right then," I said to myself. "I'm back."

When the PE lesson started, I did get nervous because I kept having flashbacks from the last game – how I'd stayed on the sidelines as soon as I'd heard "Titch" and kept dropping the ball. But I reminded myself that I was messing up because I was worrying about people laughing. I blocked it all out and focused on the game.

I was picked to play centre so had to pass the ball to Lillian and Aria, the goal attacks, to score. As soon as I began to focus on what I was doing instead of thinking about my stupid nickname, I started catching the ball and diving between players, sliding into the small spaces between them, just like when I play rugby. The fact that I was "Titch" meant I was fast and hard to stop. I passed the ball at least ten times to Lillian and Aria! We didn't end up winning because they kept missing the hoop and Sophie on the other team is so good at scoring, but it didn't matter because I felt really good. I really enjoyed the game.

I don't want to be a netball player when I'm older. I'm still set on playing rugby. But I've stopped dreading netball. The "Titch" nickname doesn't really bother me that much either anymore. I may be small, but I'm the best scrum-half in the school!

SOPHIE

I was so excited when Mrs Davies said we were playing netball again. I'm in the county team now and we practise on weekends, but I couldn't wait to play in school too.

As much as I love netball, I've had a few problems in the PE lessons at school. Mostly, it's down to one girl called Aria. We were changing for PE last week and she made some horrible comment about my size and said I looked like a boy. I might be a bit bigger than the other girls in class but I'm stronger too because I have to make sure I keep my body extra healthy for all the matches I play. I'm always full of energy! Keeping myself fit means I've built up some muscles, which I'm really proud of, but I definitely don't look like a boy!

I heard Aria and her friends sniggering when I was getting changed, which wasn't very nice. But I'm really lucky. I've got a really nice group of friends. We always stand up for each other. When my friends realized what was happening, they gathered around me and we all got changed together. We ignored Aria's group and carried on chatting! None of my group really care about what the other person looks like – we're all mates because we've all got the same sense of humour and because we're nice to each other! It makes things a lot easier! We do fall out sometimes but then we make up pretty quickly. We're always there for each other when it counts.

Aria and her friends laughing at me wasn't nice at all but I didn't let it bother me for too long. When I chatted to Mum about it she said they were probably being mean to make themselves feel better about something – maybe they had their own issues about their size or what they look like? Who knows? I've always felt really positive and confident about my body – it helps me to play netball really well after all! Mum always says it's what's inside that counts so I never really compare myself to other girls. I know I'm good enough. I guess that's why I knew I couldn't stop Aria saying whatever she wanted, but I didn't have to care about what she thought. She's not my friend after all! My friends make me feel good about myself. They're the ones I listen to! And mostly I listen to myself. I know that what I look like is just one small part of who I am and I actually like every bit that makes me, well...me!

ARIA

When I saw Sophie changing before PE it made me so mad. She's always so confident. She's really good at netball too so I could tell she couldn't wait to show off. I suck at netball.

"Wow, someone's got a bit chubby and looks even more like a boy now!" I laughed as she was getting changed.

My friends laughed, which made me feel good. Sophie's not actually chubby and doesn't look like a boy at all, but I couldn't think of anything else to say to make them laugh. Laughing at someone else gets the attention away from me while I'm changing. I've started to hate getting changed because everyone can see. Even though I try to cover up, it feels like everyone is looking and noticing what's happening to me. I'm usually quite skinny but over the last few months my body's started to change. I look all weird and curvy and I've started to get pimples on my face even though I'm not doing anything differently. When I look at Instagram, everyone looks skinny and perfect and I want to look like that. I don't want to get curvier or have pimples. I hate it. Especially because I don't know why it's happening and it doesn't seem to be happening to anyone else.

Even Dad noticed last week and made some stupid comment to Mum about me starting to grow up. It stuck in my head because I was worrying about it already, but my family don't talk about things like that. Not even Mum. She's too worried about her weight. She's always saying she's fat even though she's not. And then she tells me I'm "perfect," but I don't know what to believe anymore. It's all really confusing.

I've always thought looking good is everything. It's all I've ever been good at. When I was little everyone said how pretty I was and that stuck in my head as being the most important thing. I can't remember anyone saying how nice I was or how much they really liked my personality. I kind of wish I could just be happy with who I am, like Sophie is.

TEACHER'S NOTES

Lesson objectives

◇ To encourage children to develop a positive body image to increase self-esteem and, while feeling positive about their bodies, also to realize that what is inside is more important.

◇ To celebrate everyone's differences so that they value who they are as unique individuals.

◇ To start a discussion about puberty.

◇ To encourage children to notice and question the influence that the media has on our body image.

Fact file

The stories address several issues relating to body image including self-esteem, awareness of body diversity, what makes a healthy body, puberty and the influence of the media. Body image is our mental picture of how our body looks and how we think it is perceived by others. We can have a negative body image regardless of what we look like. A poor body image affects children's wellbeing and self-esteem, so it is important to start addressing the issue in primary schools. Hutchinson and Calland (2011; see Resources section) suggest that intervention programmes aimed at adolescents "may be too late to prevent many young people from developing a negative body image" (p.5) and they cite numerous studies reporting the high levels of body worries among younger children, some as young as six years old. Nonetheless, body confidence can be increased by encouraging children to accept that our bodies are different shapes and sizes and that we should celebrate this individuality.

Some of the exercises below aim to raise awareness of the influences that children face from parents, peers and the media (including social media), which sometimes discourage this awareness of body diversity. When children are bombarded with unrealistic images that put pressure on them to look a certain way, and they place too much emphasis on their appearance as a measure of their own self-worth, they are at risk of developing low self-esteem. For girls, being slim and pretty is often seen as the ideal, whereas being tall and muscular is often seen as the ideal for boys. Children should be encouraged to question these ideals and the body-perfect media images that have an effect on them. Awareness of how images are heavily manipulated using, for example, computer alterations and cosmetics is important as it helps children to stop comparing themselves to unattainable, manufactured ideals and, instead, to embrace the differences that make us all unique.

Aria's story shows that, as well as media images, parents can have a major impact on body image and self-worth, so it is important that they are aware of the messages they are passing on to their children. The story also shows how parents have an important role to play in children's awareness of puberty, which similarly has an impact on the child's developing body image. Before tackling the issue of body image in class, parents should be informed so that they can support these discussions at home. Some parents may want to know details of what will be covered in class.

Aria's story can be used as a starting point to begin discussions about puberty, leading to further lessons dealing with specific issues related to body changes. Talking openly about puberty makes children realize that everyone's body will change when they go through puberty and that this will happen at different rates. This relieves anxiety about changes that may seem scary to begin with, particularly, as in Aria's case, if the child is not prepared for these changes.

Comprehension activities

Harrison

1. Why do you think Harrison starts to feel bad about being shorter than his friends?

2. Why do you think he starts to play netball badly?

3. Why do you think he starts to enjoy playing netball again by the end of his story?

Sophie

1. What helped Sophie to ignore Aria's unkind comments?

2. What does Sophie say is important in her friendship group?

3. Do you think Sophie has a positive body image?

4. Healthy people can be different shapes and sizes. Do you think Sophie is healthy even though she is bigger than some of the other girls in her class? How do we know that Sophie is healthy?

5. Whose opinions does Sophie care about?

Aria

1. Why do you think Aria is unkind to Sophie?

2. Why is Aria embarrassed about getting changed before the PE lesson?

3. What do you think is happening to Aria's body?

4. Who do you think Aria could talk to about the changes she is going through?

5. Does Aria have a positive or negative body image?

6. If Aria understood that body changes and weight gain were a normal part of development, especially during puberty, do you think she would feel better about her body?

7. What has influenced her body image?

8. What has led Aria to think that "looking good is everything"?

Further activities

1. How can we look after our bodies and keep them healthy? Brainstorm with your partner and draw a mind map to show the rest of the class.

> **Teacher's note** – Make suggestions if needed; for example, exercise, what food we eat, sleep, how to keep our body clean.

2. Use these ideas to create a "How to Keep Our Bodies Healthy" poster for display in the classroom.

3. What do you think body confidence and body image are? Share ideas as a class.

> **Teacher's note** – Explain that body confidence is feeling happy about your body and body image is your idea of how your body looks rather than what it actually looks like.

4. Imagine you are friends with Harrison and you hear some of your classmates teasing him about his appearance. What could you do to help him to feel better about himself? Share ideas as a class. Now, write a list of all the things you could do if you saw someone being teased about any aspect of their appearance.

5. Do you think teasing can have an effect on how we feel about ourselves?

6. Why do you think some people say unkind things to make others feel bad about themselves?

7. Have you ever let someone's opinion of you affect what you think about yourself, like Harrison does in the story? Do you think this is a good or bad idea?

8. What advice would you give to someone who has a poor body image?

9. Without mentioning your appearance, write down a list of all your achievements and things you are good at.

10. Resources – person card cut-outs.

   On one side of the cut-out of the person, draw a portrait of the person sitting next to you. Once you have completed this, you will know one small part about their identity (their appearance) but you won't know anything about their character or what they are like as a person.

   To find out what they are like inside, ask them ten questions about themselves; for example, what do you like doing? What are your skills? What don't you like doing? Write these on the other side of the card cut-out.

   Teacher's note – Note that identity is not defined by appearance – what is inside gives us more information about the person.

11. Create a person card cut-out, as above, for yourself. Compare your cut-out with your partner's cut-out.

   Teacher's note – Note how we are all different, inside and out.

12. The teacher should read Oliver Jeffers' *The Hueys in: The New Jumper* to the class.

   a. Why do you think the Hueys are unsure about Rupert when he wears his new jumper?

   b. The Hueys are all the same. Write a short story, describing what it would be like if everyone were exactly the same, with the same personalities and appearance.

   c. Think about your class and how everyone has their own unique characteristics. Why do you think it is a good thing that everyone is unique?

d. Design your own Huey with their own unique outfit. Compare your Huey to the other Hueys in the class.

> **Teacher's note** – Note that all the Huey designs are different because we are all different.

13. Our bodies are amazing and can do amazing things. Make a list of all the things that we can do with our bodies. Now, use this list and the list you created in activity 9 to design a poster celebrating everything good about you, inside and out!

14. Hutchinson and Callard (2011) have a useful group activity exploring factors that may influence good and bad body image, and how confidence and self-esteem are more important than appearance.

15. Split the class in half. Half the class will research what women in the Victorian era considered to be beautiful. The other half of the class will research the ideal of beauty for women in Thailand's Kayan Hill tribe. Feed back what you have found to the rest of the class.

> **Teacher's note** – Highlight how beauty is a variable that changes over time and in different cultures. This can lead to discussions about how we sometimes feel pressure to look a certain way, even though what is considered beautiful is variable.

16. The class should watch "Dove Evolution" which highlights how the images we see in the media are often manipulated and enhanced (www.youtube.com/watch?v=iYhCnojf46U).

   If the image has clearly been enhanced, as many images are in the media, why is it unhelpful to compare ourselves to this image? Share ideas as a class.

17. What changes do you think happen in puberty?

18. If your friend was worried about going through puberty like Aria is, what advice could you give them? Write a script for a role play between yourself and your friend.

19. Write down a list of all the people you could talk to about the changes that everyone goes through in puberty.

RESOURCES

Books and articles
Fiction

Beaumont, K. (2010) *I Like Myself!* Boston, MA: Houghton Mifflin.

Calland, C. and Hutchinson, N. (2017) *Minnie and Max are OK!: A Story to Help Children Develop a Positive Body Image.* London and Philadelphia, PA: Jessica Kingsley Publishers.

Jeffers, O. (2012) *The Hueys in: The New Jumper.* London: HarperCollins.

Lovell, P. and Catrow, D. (2001) *Stand Tall, Molly Lou Melon.* New York: Scholastic Inc.

Richmond, M. (2015) *Hooray for You!: A Celebration of "You-Ness,"* reprint edition. Naperville, IL: Sourcebooks Jabberwocky.

Non-fiction

Birbeck, D. and Drummond, M. (2006) "Very young children's body image: bodies and minds under construction." *International Education Journal, 7*(4), 423–434.

Hutchinson, N. and Calland, C. (2011) *Body Image in the Primary School.* London and New York: Routledge.

Kostanski, M. and Gullone, E. (2007) "The impact of teasing on children's body image." *Journal of Child and Family Studies, 16,* 307–319.

Meiners, C. (2006) *Accept and Value Each Person, Learning to Get Along.* Minneapolis, MN: Free Spirit Publishing.

Richards, N. and Hague, J. (2016) *Being Me (and Loving it): Stories and Activities to Help Build Self-Esteem, Confidence, Positive Body Image and Resilience in Children.* London and Philadelphia, PA: Jessica Kingsley Publishers.

Websites

About Face www.about-face.org

> About Face is an information site for girls about the negative influence of the media and culture.

"Dove Evolution" www.youtube.com/watch?v=iYhCnojf46U

Dove School Workshops on Body Image www.dove.com/uk/dove-self-esteem-project/school-workshops-on-body-image-confident-me.html

> "Dove School Workshops on Body Image: Confident Me" (recommended for the 11–13 age group but can be used for some younger groups).

SIRC www.sirc.org/publik/mirror.html

> "Mirror Mirror: A Summary of Research Findings on Body Image."

10

Finley Worries About Climate Change

I never thought about climate change at all until this year when I saw a programme on television that showed how the world is getting hotter and hotter (I learnt some difficult new words, which I have listed at the end of my story, in case you did not know them). *Climate change* is causing so much damage to our planet. I saw huge icebergs crashing into the sea and torrential rain and hurricanes sweeping across the land. Worst of all, a lot of it is our fault!! When we burn coal, wood and gas (called *fossil fuels*) *carbon dioxide* is released into the air and this is making the world get warmer. When we drive cars or fly by aeroplane, we burn lots of these fossil fuels and release more carbon dioxide into the atmosphere. We see the results of *global warming* very often across the world with such catastrophes as forest fires, floods and hurricanes, which change the planet. The ice at the North and South Poles is melting fast and that makes the sea levels rise. Many people must leave their homes because of this global warming.

People are chopping down the rainforest and this is forcing many animals out of the *habitats* where they had always lived. Bees are also at risk because of the *chemicals* that farmers use to spray on their crops. The animals and insects suffer terribly as often they have nowhere to go, so they die or even become extinct.

Thinking about these things made me very sad. I worried about what would happen in the future to my family and friends. I worried about children in other parts of the world whose environment is changing so fast. I worried about the animals fleeing for their lives from forest fires and about polar bears stranded on the ice, with nothing to eat. I cried a lot at night when I was alone. Would we eventually have nowhere to live and have no food left? I couldn't talk about it to anyone as I was sure they would laugh at me. I just felt more and more unhappy so that in the end I didn't want to get up in the morning to go to school as it all seemed so pointless. I felt helpless. I am just a child. What could I do?

One morning, my mum noticed that my eyes were all red as I had been crying as soon as I woke up. She asked me to tell her what was making me sad. At last all my worries poured out.

I asked her, "Is there something that we can do to stop this?"

She replied, "You know, Finley, your dad and I have been worrying about the same thing too. We just didn't mention it to you as you seemed so sad and we didn't want to make you feel worse! Why don't we go and see Mrs Davies to see if she can talk to you and all the other children in your class about this very important problem and how we can try to solve it together?"

Then she told me about Greta, a Swedish girl not much older than me, who had also felt too small and helpless to do anything to solve the problem of climate change. She became very sad and lonely thinking about it, just like me, but eventually she decided to take action by entering a competition run by a Swedish newspaper to write something about climate change. For that newspaper she asked the question, "How can I feel safe when I know that we are in the greatest crisis in human history?" She won the prize! Inspired by that success, she sat outside the parliament buildings with a small sign that read "Strike for Climate!" At first, no one paid any attention, but, after a time, many children joined her protest. She became so famous that she was eventually invited to speak to important adults from all over the world about her fears for the planet. She spoke at large meetings, appeared on television and in the newspapers. She was even shortlisted for the Nobel Peace Prize!! I was amazed at how brave she is and about how she turned her sadness into action.

I said to Mum, "Perhaps we can act too!" So, Mum and I went to see Mrs Davies, who agreed that this issue is very important for all our futures. She told us that she was planning some lessons for my class on climate change and some presentations for the whole school. She also had ideas for designing a school garden where we could protect some of the wildlife that is threatened, like bees, birds, butterflies and hedgehogs. She said that children can, as Greta did, play an important part in solving the problem of climate change.

Here are some of the things that she said children and their families can do to reduce their *carbon footprint*:

- ◇ Eat less meat.

- ◇ Buy food that is grown in local farms, if possible.

- ◇ Stop using insecticides and sprays to kill flies, moths, spiders, snails and other small creatures.

- ◇ Walk, run or cycle, when possible, rather than drive.

- ◇ Recycle leftover food.

- ◇ Limit the number of plastic products in the home.

- ◇ Look after your possessions, mend them when they are broken, give them to someone else when you no longer need them.

If many people do these simple things, together we can change the world a lot and save our planet. It made me feel much happier about the future to think that every child can make a difference, wherever they are. We can also campaign to adults in power, like politicians, to make big changes in the world, as Greta did.

TEACHER'S NOTES

Lesson objectives

◇ To introduce pupils to the issue of *climate change* and why the boy in the story was so worried about its impact on our lives.

◇ To facilitate class discussion about developing empathy for people and wildlife directly affected by climate change.

◇ To empower children to understand that positive action can be taken to address this global problem.

Fact file

Scientists have identified the following useful terms:

• *Ecosystem.* This term refers to the different regions of the Earth that are made up of living things, like plants, animals and organisms that interact with one another and also interact with the environment, to include the weather, the climate, the soil, the atmosphere and the sun. There are two major types of ecosystem: *terrestrial* (land) and *aquatic* (water). The ecosystems interact with each other to create a healthy natural environment, but if one is disrupted then it can have a negative effect on the others. The problem is that humans have been doing things to the Earth that cause the ecosystems to be out of balance with one another.

• *Global warming.* The Earth is surrounded by a layer of gases called the atmosphere, which protects the Earth, absorbs heat from the sun and keeps the temperature of the Earth steady. This affects our patterns of weather and climate. But if we put too much carbon dioxide into the atmosphere, heat gets trapped and temperatures begin to rise. This is what has been happening when we humans burn fossil fuels, like coal, oil and gas, and when we damage our natural resources, like forests and oceans, or when we put harmful chemicals into the ecosystem, for example, through the use of pesticides. This leads to global warming and, as a result, climate change.

• *Climate change.* This means changes to our weather, for example, hotter summers, heavier rainfall, droughts and floods. When the seas warm up, this affects breeding areas of fish and animals, raises sea levels and causes rivers to burst their banks. This puts people who live on the coast or by rivers, as well as people who live on islands, at risk of flooding and submersion. As a result, some people have to move away from their homes as they can no longer live there.

- *Fossil fuels.* These are mainly coal, fuel oil or natural gas, formed from the remains of dead plants and animals. When we burn them, they emit greenhouse gases such as carbon dioxide, which contribute greatly to global warming.

- *Atmosphere of Earth.* According to Wikipedia, the atmosphere of the Earth protects life on Earth by creating pressure allowing for liquid water to exist on the Earth's surface, absorbing ultraviolet solar radiation, warming the surface through heat retention (greenhouse effect), and reducing temperature extremes between day and night.

- *Carbon footprint.* This is the total amount of greenhouse gases produced to directly and indirectly support human activities, usually expressed in equivalent tonnes of carbon dioxide.

Action on climate change

There are many organizations concerned about climate change, such as Greenpeace, World Wildlife Fund (WWF), Friends of the Earth and the Campaign on Climate Change, which all provide useful resources for schools to use in order to heighten children's awareness of the issues and to outline ways in which children as well as adults can take action.

In the story, Finley, a thoughtful child, was very worried after he saw a programme about climate change and saw dramatic pictures of polar ice melting and rivers bursting their banks. Understandably, he began to be fearful about the future for himself, his family and his community. He felt helpless and hopeless about what might be done to protect our planet. But through telling his mum about his fears, he began to understand that action is being taken at different levels in society and that children can play an important part in this process. Mrs Davies built on this concern by discussing her plans to create an ecology garden in the school and by planning some class lessons and assembly presentations on climate change.

Comprehension activities

1. How did Finley feel when he saw a television programme about climate change? What is climate change and why is it important to learn about it?

2. Why was it so difficult for Finley to tell anyone about his worries?

3. Why do you think that Finley felt powerless to do anything about the problem of climate change?

4. How did his mum and later Mrs Davies make him feel stronger about doing something? What do you think Finley did next?

Further activities

1. Designing a garden to protect insects. The teacher shows the class the video "Thanks for giving bees a brighter future," which demonstrates how action and campaigning made a big difference for bees in our country (https://friendsoftheearth.uk/bees/thanks-giving-bees-brighter-future). In small groups the children design a garden that protects bees and other small creatures, such as hedgehogs, squirrels, butterflies and birds.

2. How does it feel to have your home washed away or destroyed by a forest fire? The teacher shows the children video clips from the WWF or Friends of the Earth websites (e.g. www.wwf.org.uk/get-involved/schools/resources/primary-school-resources) that show animals and humans having their lives disrupted by climate change in the form of floods, storms or fires. The children write stories about a child who has this experience. What must it feel like to lose everything? What would you save if you had to escape quickly? How would you try to start again in another place?

3. What can children do? The teacher shows the class the video of Greta Thunberg giving a speech on climate change (https://www.youtube.com/watch?v=KjRDUlkEbu4). The class is divided into groups, each of which plans a presentation to give within the class or, possibly, to an assembly.

4. Protecting our own environment. In small groups, children write on large pieces of paper action that they and their families can take to protect the local environment. This can include: recycling food waste, recycling toys and clothes, changing diet and some of the ideas that Finley mentioned in the story.

RESOURCES

Books

Tucker, Z. (2019) *Greta and the Giants.* London: Frances Lincoln Children's Books.

> *Greta and the Giants*, written by Zoe Tucker and beautifully illustrated by Zoe Persico, is an inspiring story about how a child, Greta, can engage in activism and in this way have a powerful influence on how the adults (giants) treat their environment.

Rajput, M. (n.d.) *The Hat That Saved the World*. Self-published.

> *The Hat That Saved the World* is a story self-published by activist Meena to inspire children to protect the oceans and the planet. It can be ordered at https://thehatthatsavedtheworld. my-online.store

Websites

Eco Schools www.eco-schools.org.uk

> This is a global programme involving a seven-step framework that empowers children to become more aware of their environment, to develop new skills, to improve their school environment and to be proactive in driving change. Over 19.5 million children in 67 countries are engaged in this project.

Friends of the Earth www.friendsoftheearth.uk

> Friends of the Earth England, Wales and Northern Ireland is a grassroots environmental campaigning community that aims to take action on such issues as: protecting your home and local environment; adopting alternative energy solutions; and fighting for environmental and social justice globally. The website contains child-friendly videos, such as "Thanks for giving bees a brighter future," that demonstrate how action and campaigning made a big difference for bees in our country (https://friendsoftheearth.uk/ bees/thanks-giving-bees-brighter-future).

Greenpeace www.greenpeace.org.uk

> Greenpeace is an organization that raises awareness about such issues as rising sea levels, extreme weather events and the loss of biodiversity. Greenpeace campaigns internationally to challenge the action of destructive industries that threaten our forests, oceans and air. The website has lots of information about threatened species, such as turtles, whales and penguins, and describes what Greenpeace is doing to protect our natural world for future generations.

Greta Thunberg is a young Swedish environmental activist, born in 2003, whose campaigning has gained international recognition. To read about her life, look her up online. In particular, look for a video of Greta speaking at the 2019 World Economic Forum in Davos (https:// www.youtube.com/watch?v=KjRDUlkEbu4).

The Campaign against Climate Change www.campaigncc.org

> The Campaign against Climate Change is an organization that brings people together to push for the urgent and resolute action we need to prevent the catastrophic destabilization of global climate. It has a valuable section on its website on the theme of climate change education in schools. This recognizes that children are very concerned about the climate

crisis and angry that not enough is being done about it by adults. The resources provided here are designed for children and young people at different stages of their education. There is also information on *Teach the Future*, a youth-led campaign to focus the educational system around the crisis of climate change.

WWF www.worldwildlife.org

For over 60 years, WWF, the world's leading conservation organization, has worked and campaigned to help people and wildlife thrive. WWF works internationally to collaborate with people around the world to develop and deliver innovative solutions that protect communities, wildlife and the places in which they live. WWF has a wealth of photos and videos on the six major aspects of their work: climate, food, forests, fresh water, oceans and wildlife. WWF has a range of inspiring activities for primary schools at www.wwf.org. uk/get-involved/schools/resources/primary-school-resources and on how to develop a plastic-free school at www.sas.org.uk/plastic-free-schools

For more information about their work on engaging with children and young people, see www.wwf.org.uk/get-involved/youth-engagement

11

Mason Has Motor Difficulties

"Time for drama," said Mrs Davies. "Let's line up."

I love drama. I am really good at imagining stories and showing how I feel in my face. But to get to the hall where we do drama is another story. I can't even walk down the corridor without tripping and bumping into things. When I walk down the corridor at school and children are walking all around in what seems like different directions, I really need to focus or else I will trip. Today, my friends Niall and Jamie were walking on either side of me and chatting. Niall made a joke about something he had watched on the telly last night. I didn't really hear him because I was concentrating so hard on not tripping. I really wish I could focus on what my friends are saying and walking down the corridor at the same time. It just doesn't seem fair. It's hard for me to remember things when I am doing something like walking down the corridor. I'm even worse at sport. I hate PE because when we play football or rugby or anything with a ball, I can't even figure out where the ball is coming from and which direction it is supposed to be going in.

Luckily, today, we were doing drama. It's a bit hard for me to start to remember my lines. Once I practise them for a long time with my dad, I never forget them. It's when I need to remember things on the spot that I forget. Sometimes, people think I am scatty, but I just need to concentrate more. Luckily, Dad and I had practised my lines for hours last night. The play is all about what's going to happen to the Earth if we don't change. I pretended I was the Earth and he was a polar bear. I am so excited because I get to be the Earth. It's amazing all the things that people are doing to the Earth. I felt so sad practising my lines. But I am also happy that we will do this play.

And it's easy for me to act as someone who is sad because I am sad at all the things I miss out on, like cricket and football, at school. I am also always last to be picked for teams at PE. And I don't go to birthday parties if they are any kind of sport parties. Last week, Niall had a bowling party. I am sure it was fun, but I told my mum I didn't want to go. My mum is wicked. She told his mum that we were away, but that we would be back in time for the food bit. That was really fun because I like joking around with my friends. I have a book of jokes and I always learn them.

Anyway, we got to drama and needed to change into our drama costumes. My mum has sewn Velcro into my shirt so I don't have to do the buttons. I didn't want anyone to see that she had done this. It takes me forever to do buttons. I would always be the last one to get ready. I pretended I needed the toilet and changed there. My dad searched everywhere and found these laces that look like real laces even though I don't have to tie them. My dad is wicked.

We were acting out the story of the Earth for a learning assembly in front of our parents. I just have to be sad and say my lines about humans not being nice. I always remember my lines so I am not afraid of forgetting them. I love being the lead. I also love acting because I don't have to think on the spot. It's also easier than other things we do in schools because I know exactly where people are so I don't have to concentrate on not bumping into people.

We're doing this play because Finley got really upset one day at school. He's not my best mate, but he's alright. One day, Mrs Davies said we all needed to talk. She let Finley talk first. He looked upset and I first thought he was such a swot! But then he started talking about the climate crisis and the polar bears with nothing to eat and I got scared. I was afraid that we wouldn't have enough to eat if things changed too fast. Mrs Davies asked if we had suggestions. I raised my hand and asked Mrs Davies if we could do a play on the climate crisis for our learning assembly for our parents. I really wanted to do a play because it's something I am good at. The whole class thought that this was a good idea. She said we should think about all the things that we needed to tell the grown-ups so that they would "change their behaviour." We started coming up with a list and then Mrs Davies wrote everything down. I felt really good about myself that I could come up with an idea and that Mrs Davies and the whole class thought it was a good idea.

TEACHER'S NOTES

Lesson objectives

⋄ To understand difficulties faced by children with motor difficulties and, in particular, developmental coordination disorder (DCD).

Fact file

What is DCD? It is a neurological condition that affects movement, which is diagnosed on the basis of significant motor coordination impairments. People often use the term interchangeably with dyspraxia, but DCD is the formal diagnosis. Often children with DCD show delays in reaching developmental milestones (e.g. sitting up, crawling). Children with DCD may appear clumsy. They may have problems with fine motor skills (e.g. tying shoes), gross motor skills (e.g. kicking a ball) or both. DCD has a prevalence of around 5 per cent (i.e. at least one child in every classroom). It can also affect short-term memory, planning, dressing or riding a bike.

Because tasks that involve motor activities may fatigue children, they may not have the necessary resources for other skills. They may also avoid activities that involve motor skills (e.g. sport, arts and crafts) with their peers. Perhaps as a result, children with DCD often have poor social skills and social understanding, low self-esteem and emotion understanding, and high levels of anxiety and depression.

Help and support for children and young people with DCD

Typically occupational therapists and educational psychologists can help children with DCD. They try to develop strategies in the home and at school (e.g. using technology rather than writing) that can help children adapt to their environments. They may also teach specific motor skills tasks that the child finds difficult.

For example, in the story Mason was vulnerable because he had to concentrate so hard on walking around the school without tripping or falling. But by building on his passion for drama, Mrs Davies was able to take up his idea for a play on climate change and involve him closely with his peer group in its planning and performance in an activity that did not involve motor skills. Like many children with DCD, Mason has some difficulty with working memory, which was seen in his difficulty in learning his lines. Once he had learnt them, however, he would not forget them because children with DCD do not typically have difficulty with long-term memory.

Comprehension activities

In pairs, discuss the following questions:

1. In the story, how does Mason's mother help him to cope at school? Can you think of other difficulties he may have?

2. Which types of activities does he miss?

3. What strengths does he have?

Further activities

1. Can you come up with adaptations (changes) for him? For example, if he has difficulty writing, could he use a tablet? What if other children were jealous?

2. What types of activities could you do to include someone like Mason in your play?

3. Some famous people who have been diagnosed with DCD include Daniel Radcliffe (actor), Emma Louise Lewell-Buck (MP), Florence Welsh (singer) and Ellis Genge (rugby player). Choose one of these famous people. In pairs, write a story about how DCD may have affected them as children.

4. What other conditions may affect movement? How might these be similar or different to DCD?

RESOURCES

There is Dyspraxia Awareness Week each year.

British Dyslexia Association www.bdadyslexia.org.uk/dyslexia/neurodiversity-and-co-occurring-differences/dyspraxia

British Dyslexia Association has information about different neurodiversity including DCD.

Dyspraxia Foundation https://dyspraxiafoundation.org.uk/about-dyspraxia/information-sheets/?gclid=CjwKCAiA44LzBRB-EiwA-jJipCLEoHWgJ61WR8SbeuLZtjHzHiLPpXzfcdX2FjPUqVRtpYZK9M9_RxoCnsEQAvD_BwE

Dyspraxia Foundation, a small charity, provides information for parents, professionals, and adults and children with dyspraxia and DCD. Dyspraxia Foundation has an annual conference. The website discusses differences between dyspraxia in children and adults. It also has local groups.

Movement Matters www.movementmattersuk.org

Movement Matters is a website funded by the Waterloo Foundation that provides information about the diagnosis of DCD.

NHS www.nhs.uk/conditions/developmental-coordination-disorder-dyspraxia/symptoms

The NHS website provides an overview of DCD, its symptoms, diagnosis and treatment.

SUMMER TERM

12

Miriam's Parents Are Going Through a Divorce

Our "All About Me" project was really fun. We'd done a presentation about our hobbies and loads of artwork to show our personalities. But then Mrs Davies said that we were going to be writing about our families. My heart sank.

My family used to be like everyone else's family, but then everything changed. I guess Mum and Dad had been arguing a lot, but I couldn't believe it when they said they were getting divorced. None of my best friends' parents are divorced. Just mine. I was so angry and upset that I thought I'd never stop crying.

Sometimes, they'd argued when I'd been naughty, so at first I thought it was my fault. They sat me down and explained, "It's nothing to do with you, Miriam, and it's definitely not your fault." They said people get divorced when they stop loving each other. But then I thought: if they can stop loving each other, could they stop loving me? Mum could tell I was upset and told me there was nothing that would stop them from loving me. I knew deep down that was true, but it all felt really confusing.

"I want you to draw a portrait of your family and write at least three sentences about why your family is special," Mrs Davies said.

We were meant to present it in front of the whole class! I was dreading it so much I felt sick. My family was split up so was it still a family? I didn't know where to start.

I stared at the blank piece of paper in front of me and felt really alone. Most of the class seemed to be getting on with their drawings without a worry in the world. I glanced over at my best friend's picture. She'd drawn her mum, dad and brother all together in one house. Suddenly, I felt really sad and panic started to tighten in my stomach. I didn't know why our family was special. I couldn't think of one sentence, never mind three.

When it was time to present, Mrs Davies asked who wanted to go first. I sank into my seat.

Abigail put her hand up straight away. She loves presenting in front of the class, whatever topic we're doing.

"This is my picture," she said in a loud, confident voice. "Here's me and my little brother outside our house and here's our mums inside, watching television. One mum is wearing her uniform because she's a nurse and my other mum is in her normal clothes because she owns a shop. Our family is really special because we all love each other and make each other laugh. Apart from my brother. He's really annoying."

We all laughed. I started to feel more relaxed and sat up a little in my chair. Maybe I wasn't the only one with a different family.

Abigail sat down and Mrs Davies chose the next person to speak.

Isaac came to the front and held up his picture.

"This is Mum and Dad with our pet dog Tiger. Mum and Dad flew all the way to India to adopt me. Our family is special because they wanted me so much that they flew all that way. And Tiger is special because he licks my face."

I knew that Isaac was adopted but I hadn't really thought about it too much before. It was pretty cool that his mum and dad had flown all that way. I guess his family was different too.

Next Niall put his hand up. We all felt really sad for Niall because his dad had died over the summer.

"This is me and my mum in our house. I've drawn Dad here too because he'll always be my dad. In the garden I've drawn all my cousins, aunties and uncles because they're always popping round for barbeques. It's nice having a big family who look out for each other. That's why we're special."

Mrs Davies thanked Niall and gave him a big smile. I thought he was really brave for showing his picture. Maybe I could be brave like him and show my picture too. And maybe I did have something I could write about. I picked up my pencil as Kerry went to the front to present.

"This is my mum and my brother Danny. I don't see my dad. My family is special because we give each other hugs."

Maybe Kerry was right and giving each other hugs was special. Mum and Dad are always hugging me, even when I'm busy doing something else! I quickly scribbled something down as Makai got up to present.

"This is me, my sister and my foster dads," he said, holding up his picture. "My mum couldn't look after us properly, which made me really mad at first. But now I'm getting happier. My foster dads are really nice. Our family is special because we care about each other."

Makai's picture was so colourful and he'd drawn big smiles on everyone's faces. I quickly added big smiles to everyone in my picture.

"Miriam?" asked Mrs Davies. "Are you ready for your turn?"

I had butterflies in my stomach and my fists were clenched but I figured if the rest of the class could do it, then so could I. I went to the front of the class and nervously held up my picture.

"This is my family. Mum lives in this house and Dad lives in this one. Sometimes, I wish we were all still together, but it works better for us this way. Now there's no more arguing. I thought my family was the only one that was different but I think everyone's family can be different in some way. I guess it's not a bad thing. So, I've written, 'My family is special because Mum and Dad love me very much. And that's the most important thing.'"

TEACHER'S NOTES

Lesson objectives

- ◇ To make children aware of different kinds of family structures and to encourage understanding, acceptance and respect for these differences.

- ◇ To celebrate each child's unique family and recognize that every family is special.

- ◇ To recognize similarities and differences between families and that love and caring are common characteristics within many families.

Fact file

The story shows a wide variety of diverse family structures both to encourage children to appreciate and understand differences in the families of their peers and to enable them to find themselves in the story, thereby developing pride in their own family. The story emphasizes that "family" can mean different things to different people, even within one classroom. This encourages tolerance as children appreciate that every family is unique. Children should be encouraged to notice that the common theme within all the families in the story, whatever the configuration, is love.

Prior to the lesson, it is a good idea to consult with families to check how they refer to their own family and to discuss any concerns. For example, you may want to address any special concerns that families who have suffered a bereavement or have adopted or fostered children or are dealing with other issues such as divorce may have about the topic. The important thing is that all children in the classroom feel included and positive about the topic.

Comprehension activities

1. In the story, there are many different types of families. Do any of the families look like your family?

2. What do you think is a common characteristic in many of the families portrayed in the story?

3. Why do you think Miriam is nervous about telling the rest of the class about her family?

4. What does Miriam realize at the end of the story?

Further activities

1. What is a family? Write your thoughts into a mind map. Remember to spread your lines and words out.

    > **Teacher's note** – Emphasize that people define families in different ways and that each family is unique.

2. Make a quick sketch of what you think a "typical" family looks like.

    > **Teacher's note** – Explain that families come in different shapes and sizes so drawing a typical family is very difficult.

3. What do you think is an important element in a happy family? Discuss in pairs and feed back to the rest of the class.

4. Make a list of all the people who could be in a family.

5. What does your family look like? Draw a portrait of the people who love and care for you and write a few sentences about what makes your family special. It is your choice who to include because "family" means different things to different people.

    > **Teacher's note** – Create a gallery of the portraits as a visual reminder of the different types of family that there are in the classroom.

6. Why do you think we should learn about different sorts of families? Do you think it's important to accept these differences? Discuss in groups and feed back to the rest of the class.

7. Divide your paper into two columns. With your partner, talk about your families. In one column write down three things that are the same about your families. In the other column write down three things that are different. Feed back to the rest of the class.

RESOURCES

Books
Fiction

Coffelt, N. and Tusa, T. (2008) *Fred Stays with Me*. New York: Little, Brown Young Readers.

Harris, R. (2015) *Who's in My Family?: All about Our Families*. London: Walker Books.

Hoffman, M. and Asquith, R. (2015) *The Great Big Book of Families*. London: Frances Lincoln Children's Books.

Lang, S. and Lang, M. (2015) *Families, Families, Families*. London: Picture Corgi.

Lopez, S. and Chen, Z. (2018) *Just Right Family, An Adoption Story*. Park Ridge, IL: Albert Whitman & Company.

Masurel, C. and Denton, K. (2002) *Two Homes*, new edition. London: Walker Books.

O'Leary, S. and Leng, Q. (2016) A *Family is a Family is a Family*. Toronto: Groundwood Books.

Parr, T. (2010) *The Family Book*, reprint edition. New York: Little, Brown Young Readers.

Rotner, S. and Kelly, S. (2015) *Families*. New York: Holiday House.

Schiffer, M. and Clifton-Brown, H. (2015) *Stella Brings the Family*, 1st edition. San Francisco, CA: Chronicle Books.

Non-fiction

Derman-Sparks, L. and Edwards, J.O. (2019) *Anti-Bias Education for Young Children and Ourselves*, 2nd revised edition. Washington DC: National Association for the Education of Young Children.

Websites

Welcoming Schools www.welcomingschools.org/resources/books/diverse-families

www.welcomingschools.org/resources/lesson-plans/diverse-families/diverse-families-with-books

> Welcoming Schools has a list of recommended fiction books and some simple accompanying lessons plans, introducing diversity in families.

13

Molly Is Not a Stereotypical Girl

My name is Molly. I've always loved playing football. I play centre midfield for an academy. In the last game, I scored three goals. I also like playing rugby and cricket in PE.

Every week, my dad drives me to the academy. It's quite a long drive because there aren't a lot of academies for girls. It's great being with him because he tells me all about his job as an engineer. It sounds so interesting. He once even helped me build my own computer. I really want to be like my dad when I grow up.

At the beginning of last year, the boys at school wouldn't let me play football at break times with them. They kept saying football was for boys. Our head teacher told them that she would ban football at break time if they didn't start including everyone who wanted to play. This made them let me join in, but they never passed the ball to me, especially if Felix was playing. He's amazing at football. One day though, Felix was at a tennis competition all day. Jamie passed the ball to me and I hit the crossbar and it went in. It was the best goal of my life. After that, Jamie, Felix and Niall let me play football with them. Now, I play football with them every day.

I was so happy. I wanted to play better and better. I asked my mum to let me wear my brother's trousers to school. I asked her to buy me black lace shoes instead of those horrible girls' shoes. You can't play football in them. They just come off when you get tackled. My mum was not happy. She said that I'd look like a boy if I wore trousers. My mum always says I look like a right mess. She works in a salon cutting hair. She finally agreed to get me new shoes when I showed her the massive bruise on my leg I got after my shoe fell off when I was tackled. She also doesn't like it when my hair gets all messed up when I play, especially after she's taken ages making it look nice. I really like having my hair done by Mum. But now she kept getting annoyed so home was not so fun.

And then once I started playing football, Niamh and Yasmin stopped sitting with me at lunch. They seemed annoyed too. I didn't understand it. I asked them why and they told me that it was because I was not a "real girl." They also said that I looked silly in those boys' clothes. I still liked talking to girls and having friends who are girls, but I wanted to play football. They were my best friends so then I didn't really have anyone to sit with at lunch. They didn't invite me to their houses or birthday parties anymore. I really missed having them as friends and didn't understand why we couldn't play after school. Even if I like some boy things, I still wanted to be their friend. And I really like it when we do arts and crafts at their parties. I like loads of girl things. It's not only boy things I like. And it's silly to say things are only for girls or boys anyway.

Jamie, Felix and Niall didn't invite me to their birthday parties either because they only invited the boys. I heard Felix telling Niall that his mother said that he could pick his six best friends to go to the park for a football match for his birthday. He said he couldn't invite me because his mother said that I wouldn't enjoy the party because I am a girl. But that's not true! I know as much about football as any of them.

Even though they let me play football with them at break times, the boys didn't sit next to me at lunch either. I was sitting alone one day, when our PE teacher, Mr Ayling, walked by.

"Why are you alone, Molly?" he asked.

I mumbled something.

"But I always see you play football with Jamie and Felix at break time," he replied. "Why don't you just go sit with them?"

I really didn't know what to say.

"Follow me," he said. I followed him to where Jamie was sat.

"Listen, mates. Do you think Molly could eat lunch with you?"

"Uh, okay," said Jamie.

"Okay," said Felix.

From that day on, I always sat with them. I didn't realize that I could have just asked them. But I still missed Niamh and Yasmin.

At least I have friends outside school. I get on with the girls at the academy and we play football together. We even go on trips together each summer to play football. Last year, we even went to Denmark to play in a massive tournament. It was so much fun!!

TEACHER'S NOTES

Lesson objectives

⬦ To teach children that stereotypes are often inaccurate and that many children enjoy doing activities stereotyped for both genders.

⬦ To learn that boys and girls, women and men, are more similar than different.

Fact file

Many children have interests that include activities and toys that are stereotyped for the other gender. Unfortunately for many of these children, lots of research studies indicate that other children are more likely to reject children who are perceived as having gender-atypical interests. Children often believe that they should select children for activities that match the gender stereotype of the activities. In other words, if asked to choose a girl or a boy to play netball, children will more likely select a girl than a boy. Another research finding is that when a child has interests stereotyped for the other gender, children assume that all their interests match the other gender.

Help and support for children and young people who cross gender boundaries

Teachers and parents can be aware that some children have interests that span across gender and try to make sure that children who have interests stereotyped for the other gender do not feel excluded.

In the story, Molly lost friendships with some girls like Niamh and Yasmin who stopped playing with her because, in their words, she was "not a real girl." Initially, the boys wouldn't play with her either at break time as, in their words, "football is for boys." Following patterns found in research studies, the children rejected a child who had atypical interests. The girls didn't invite her to parties and neither did the boys. Even the parents reinforced these stereotypes. But Molly has lots of interests, like arts and crafts. She also loves playing competitively in girls' football tournaments. She is lively and sociable. Luckily, Mr Ayling encouraged her to ask Jamie and Felix if she could sit with them at lunch time and that worked out very well.

Comprehension activities

1. Can you think of a way that the other characters use stereotypes of Molly?

2. In what way are these stereotypes incorrect?

3. What would you do differently if you were in Molly's class?

Further activities

Stereotypes

Objective: To teach children what a stereotype is and to demonstrate that stereotypes are not always accurate.

Stereotype: what we think about a group of people (e.g. girls, boys, adults) that may not be true. We think it is true about every person in that group.

1. In pairs, research a famous female scientist. Feed back to the rest of the class. In pairs, research a famous male nurse. Feed back to the rest of the class.

> **Teacher's note** – For this activity you could divide the class into mixed pairs to encourage the sharing of ideas.

2. Often we have stereotypes about the emotions that women and men, girls and boys show. For example, sometimes people think that men do not cry and feel sad, or that women do not feel anger. Think of a time your mother was angry or your father was sad.

> **Teacher's note** – For this part, you could show children part of *Inside Out*, a film by Pixar (the trailer is here: www.youtube.com/ watch?v=seMwpPoyeu4). Which emotions does Riley express? Have you ever felt anger, fear or sadness?

3. Write a comic strip about a boy who feels sad or afraid or a girl who feels angry. www.teachers.org.uk/equality/equality-matters/breaking-mould has a series of resources to challenge traditional stereotypes.

4. Watch the Newsround episode on gender and toys (www.bbc.co.uk/ newsround/24211824). Do you think labelling toys as for girls or boys could affect which toys children play with? Do you ever play with toys that would be labelled for the other gender? In pairs, could you write a letter to a toy company explaining why they should not label toys for girls or for boys?

RESOURCES

Let Toys Be Toys http://lettoysbetoys.org.uk/ten-ways-to-challenge-gender-stereotypes-in-the-classroom

The Let Toys Be Toys campaign is asking the toy and publishing industries to stop limiting children's interests by promoting some toys and books as only suitable for girls, and others only for boys. The website has many different lesson plans for all ages. They also have lists of books that promote positive attitudes towards all children regardless of their gender (http://lettoysbetoys.org.uk/books-for-young-children-2gift-guide).

The Fawcett Society www.fawcettsociety.org.uk/smashstereotypes

The Fawcett Society is a charity that campaigns for women's equality. One of their campaigns is about challenging gender stereotypes that are harmful for children and adults.

14

Jakub Is From Poland

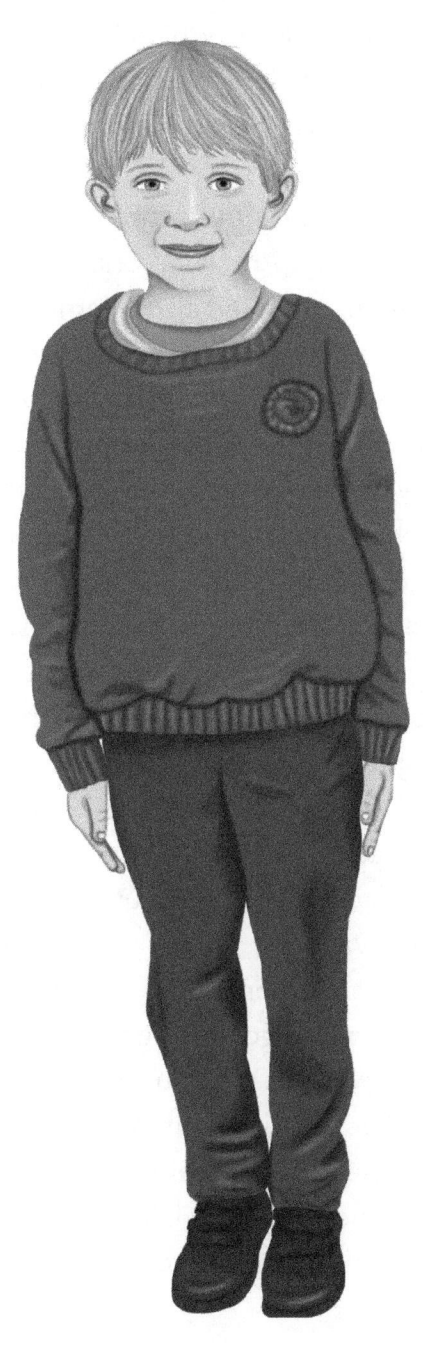

My name is Jakub and I am from Poland. I moved to the UK two years ago. It was really hard to move away from Poland where my grandmum, granddad, aunts, uncles and cousins live. My mum and dad wanted to move because they heard that there were more jobs in the UK than in Poland. In Poland, my mum was a teacher and my dad had gone to school to be an engineer. But my dad had problems finding a good job. My parents decided that we should move to the UK so that they could make more money and me and my brother could learn English. I was really sad because I had a lot of family in Poland.

When we first moved, we moved to a small town. My mum became a nanny for a family who lived in the next town. She would collect us from school with the baby and then we would go to the family's house. The baby was cute, but he wasn't old enough to play with for much time.

My dad found a job as an electrician, which is not quite what he did in Poland, but he seemed happy. My dad was less worried because he had found work. We didn't see him a lot though because he left for work early in the morning and got home late.

It was really hard for me because I was the only person in my whole school who was from a different country. And everyone had been in the same class for ages so they already had friends. I missed all my family and friends back in Poland. I had no one to sit with at lunch or to talk to. Sometimes I would try to play with other children, but no one would play with me. The only thing I liked about that place was that it was in the country so it was very green. We rented a house with a massive garden. I could play outside with my brother, but I didn't know anyone else.

I did not understand what was happening in school. I would try to listen, but it made no sense at all. Luckily, on the weekends, my mother would take me to a Polish school so I would not forget how to read and write in Polish. There were only six other kids there, but they were friendly and I had someone to talk to there. They had all been born in the UK so their Polish was not so great, but they spoke English so they taught me some words. I loved to see Mateusz and Adam each week at Polish school. We even had sleepovers and they invited me to their birthday parties. I was still sad and lonely during the week, but I knew that there was nothing my mum and dad could do because the only people they knew had kids at the Polish school anyway.

My mum and dad said that we were going to Poland for the Easter break and, when we came back, my mum was going to get a job as a teaching assistant in a new school. The new school was not near our house so we would need to move. I didn't mind at all because I had no friends in my school anyway. And I would keep going to Polish school because it was closer to where we were moving anyway.

When I started at this school, I could tell it was different from my old school. I could also speak a bit more English so that probably helped. I wasn't the only person learning English. There was also Hind. But there was something even better that I found out about on my first day!

"Children," Mrs Davies said. "I'd like you to meet Jakub, who has just moved here from Poland. What do we know about Poland?"

"One of the schools we wrote that story with are from Poland," said Felix.

"They're from Krakow," said someone else.

"Are you from Krakow?" someone asked me.

"No, I am from Warsaw. It's far away," I said. I was so excited that someone spoke to me.

"I have never been to Krakow," I said.

"In what ways are all the children the same in all the places?" asked Mrs Davies.

"All the kids are friendly," said Holly.

"And one had a puppy just like me," said Mason.

I didn't understand at first what Felix was saying about writing a story, but I didn't mind. I was just so happy someone spoke to me.

Mrs Davies explained that five classrooms from different schools, including our own, had written a story that took place in each person's town. The other classrooms were in Poland, Romania, Norway and Spain.

Then Mrs Davies said, "We also send postcards. And we get lots of postcards from children in other schools. Should we look at our map and see if we got one from Poland?"

She went over to a map where there were strings linking places on the map to postcards. "Look, we don't have one from Poland. Jakub, could you ask someone you know to send one?"

"Of course," I said.

"Can someone sit with Jakub for lunch?" Mrs Davies asked.

I couldn't believe it when five hands went up. I could tell that I was going to like my new school.

TEACHER'S NOTES

Lesson objectives

◇ To teach children that there are many similarities between children wherever they live in the world.

◇ To develop children's understanding of immigration.

Fact file

There are many immigrant children in the UK. Recent reports suggest that there are about 900,000 from non-Irish European Union countries alone (The Migration Observatory, 2018). There are also many children born to parents without UK citizenship attending schools in the UK.

Help and support for children and young people who are immigrants

Researchers often find that when people from different groups make contact with each other it can reduce prejudice. However, schools may not have lots of children from different backgrounds so children do not have opportunities to learn about children and others from different cultures. Because there were not lots of children from different countries, Mrs Davies did an etwinning project – this is an online platform that allows schools in different European countries to work together. Contact does not have to be in person. In fact, reading stories about people and then leading children to think about people from other places, called imaginary contact, can sometimes reduce prejudice.

Comprehension activities

In the story, Jakub attends two different schools. Although he is the only Polish child in both schools, the teacher in the second school had made sure that the children had opportunities for contact with children from other countries.

1. Explain to your pupils what contact is.

2. Ask the children to explain the different ways that children in the second school had opportunities for contact. Remind them that reading stories about other people and imagining that they are friends with the children can be a form of contact.

3. Ask them to explain why reading stories about children from different places might help to reduce prejudice.

Further activities

1. Ask your pupils to generate other means of contact. Remind them that reading stories about other people and imagining that they are friends with the children can be a form of contact. Ask them to explain why contact is effective for reducing prejudice.

2. Have students write a story about a child who encounters someone from a different culture and how that affects their perceptions of that culture. Remember that it is okay to discuss difference and when adults refuse to discuss difference, such as ethnicity, children begin to think it is taboo.

RESOURCES

British Council www.britishcouncil.org/etwinning/what

> British Council, which is an organization devoted to cultural relations and education, has a platform where schools can join in etwinning with other schools. Examples of successful etwinning projects may be found here: https://www.britishcouncil.org/etwinning/what/case-study

Globe Smart Kids https://globesmartkids.org

> Globe Smart Kids is a charity that focuses on teaching children about other children from diverse backgrounds. It uses ideas of contact, both real and imagined, to help children learn about others from diverse backgrounds.

Show Racism the Red Card www.theredcard.org

> Show Racism the Red Card is an anti-racism charity. They have short films by football players and work with children and schools.

The Linking Network https://thelinkingnetwork.org.uk/about

> The Linking Network is a charity that helps schools and teachers help children learn about diversity and equality. The main way that they achieve these goals is by linking two classrooms in different UK schools that differ based on demographics factors. Its website has ways to sign up as a classroom. It can also train schools and conduct continuing professional development and inset days on these topics.

Western Justice Center www.schooltools.info

> Western Justice Center has lesson plan ideas and video resources aimed at reducing prejudice.

15

Hind Is a Refugee

My first day of school was really scary. Before going I was excited because I wanted to learn new things and make new friends. I didn't have any friends in the UK. In the camp in Lebanon, where I was born, I had loads of friends. We used to play together all the time. It wasn't a very nice place to live though. It was always cold at night and everything was dirty. The worse thing was that everyone seemed sad all the time. I think they all missed their homes in Syria. That's near Lebanon and where Mum and Dad are from.

Mum and Dad had to go to the camp after escaping from Syria. There was nowhere else to go. They ran away in the middle of the night because their house was being bombed. Mum says they didn't have anything when they arrived at the camp because they had to leave everything behind. Mum explained that being a refugee is when a family, like ours, has to run away from their home because of war or fighting to find safety somewhere else. That's why my family had to leave Syria and come to the UK.

When we moved here, we didn't know anyone. I felt really lonely so I was happy when Mum and Dad told me that I would make new friends in the new school. My parents want me to study really hard because they studied really hard in Syria. They were both doctors but they can't work in the UK yet. They go to English class a few hours each day because they want to learn English. They said I'd learn English too in my new school.

I was excited to begin with, but when I actually arrived at school it was so scary because everything was different and I couldn't speak any English. I only knew a few words like "yes" and "no." I felt embarrassed and just stayed quiet all day. I'm quite loud at home and Mum used to say I was confident, but suddenly I felt shy and nervous. I had no one to play with because I couldn't speak to anyone. Even if they asked me questions, I couldn't answer back.

At lunch break, I watched the other children play and missed my friends in the camp like Aaliyah and Reem. If they were here with me, we could play together.

Everyone seemed to be in a group already. That made it hard to fit in. I think being new is hard anyway, but if you can't speak English, it's even harder. I felt really uncomfortable not being able to understand what people were saying. I think a lot of the children were whispering about me in a mean way because they kept looking at me and then laughing and turning away. I'm not sure why. But it made me feel even more lonely. I don't think I ate any of my school dinner that first day. I just moved it around the plate and squashed it onto the side. I felt so lonely and nervous that I didn't feel hungry. One girl from my class did smile at me when I was sitting on my own in the lunch hall, but I didn't know what she was saying to me, so I just kept looking down at the table.

When we got back to class, I tried to do what the other children did. When the teacher wrote maths problems on the whiteboard, I knew the answers, but didn't know how to say the answers in English. It made me feel so frustrated. It wasn't the best first day.

After school, when I got home, I didn't want to tell Mum and Dad that I didn't play with anyone because I didn't want them to worry. I wasn't looking forward to going back to school the next day. It made me feel panicky.

When I arrived at school, the girl who had smiled on my first day looked at me and smiled again. I found out her name was Cerys. I was relieved that someone was smiling because most of the other children were already busy playing together in their groups. Some of the children kept looking at me in an angry way. At least Cerys was still smiling but I was scared she would come over and try to talk to me and I wouldn't be able to say anything back. I really wanted to make friends but I didn't know how.

I don't think I said any words in school for a long time. I started to get used to sitting on my own at play times. I kind of got used to feeling lonely. I gradually started to understand what people were saying though – you have to learn pretty fast when everyone is talking in English all the time! I wasn't confident enough to say anything back yet, but it did feel a bit better being able to understand how things worked in school and what I was meant to be doing.

One morning, in assembly the head teacher said that Mrs Davies had a really exciting announcement. She said that our class was going to be doing a gardening project. Mum and Dad used to have a big garden in Syria. Our flat doesn't have a garden, so I was really excited. We had to plan everything out and all work together to decide on what we wanted to plant in the garden. I came up with some good ideas and some of the children who had always looked at me angrily smiled at me a bit. You wouldn't believe how happy that made me feel! When we were doing the project, it started to feel like I belonged to the group for the first time.

I looked forward to going out to work on the garden every week. One morning, when we were there, Cerys came over to ask if I wanted to play with her and her friends at play time. I thought she'd given up trying to make friends with me. I was so happy she asked. It was so nice to play with them and not be stuck on my own. For the first time since moving here, I felt the same as everyone else.

TEACHER'S NOTES

Lesson objectives

- ◇ To introduce pupils to the issue of refugees and to help them imagine what life is like for many child refugees.

- ◇ To encourage pupils to feel empathy for others.

- ◇ To explore myths and perceptions surrounding refugees.

- ◇ To understand that refugees arriving in the UK often face prejudice.

Fact file

Definitions

A *refugee* is someone who has been forced to leave their country, often without warning, because it is no longer safe for them to live there. They may be escaping war, violence or persecution (e.g. because of their ethnicity or political or religious beliefs). Refugee status means they have the legal right to reside safely in that country. An *asylum seeker* also flees their home because it is no longer safe for them to live there. They are waiting for their application for asylum (safety) to be considered in the hope that they will be given refugee status.

Syria: In the story, Hind's parents flee from Syria. A civil war broke out in Syria in March 2011. Like Hind's parents, millions of Syrians fled to neighbouring countries such as Lebanon. Many of these people were women and children like Hind. Since then, many have made the dangerous journey from Syria and neighbouring countries to Europe.

Comprehension activities

1. How does Hind feel when she moves to the UK? Why do you think she feels this way?

2. What do you think her parents miss about their home in Syria?

3. What do you think about the way people treat Hind when she starts school?

Further activities

1. In pairs, brainstorm what you think a "refugee" is. Try to reach agreement with your partner and write down your own definition. Feed back to the rest of the class.

> **Teacher's note** – Following this activity, ask the pupils if they know the difference between a refugee and an asylum seeker. Explain the difference.

2. Hind's family had to leave everything behind when they ran away from their home in Syria. Imagine having to leave home suddenly and move to another country. Write a first-person narrative describing how you would feel and what you would miss from home.

3. Most people usually have a choice about moving house and have time to pack. Imagine you were moving house and had lots of time to pack your things. Draw a picture of yourself with all the things that you would pack. Describe how you are feeling in the picture.

> **Teacher's note** – Explain that moving can create different feelings such as excitement and nervousness.

4. Now, imagine you have to leave your home in a hurry and can only take one small item with you. What would you take? Draw a picture of yourself with your item and describe why you would take this. Describe how you are feeling in this picture.

> **Teacher's note** – Explain that many refugees had to run from their houses with only the few personal items they could carry.

5. Imagine starting a new school and not being able to speak the language. How would you feel? Create a spider diagram to show your emotions and thoughts.

6. Imagine a new pupil like Hind was starting in your class. Make a poster to display in your classroom to demonstrate all the things you could do to make them feel welcome and included.

7. In Hind's story, some children are not very kind to Hind. Discuss in pairs why you think this might be. Feed back to the rest of the class.

8. The teacher should ask pupils if they have seen any negative representations of refugees or asylum seekers. The teacher should source examples of negative media representations of refugees and asylum seekers and ask pupils if they think these representations are fair. Ask pupils what their perception of refugees is since reading Hind's story and exploring the issue in class.

9. Write down three things you have learnt since exploring this topic in class.

RESOURCES

Books
Fiction

Bruton, C. (2019) *No Ballet Shoes in Syria*. London: Nosy Crow.

Hoffman, M. (2003) *The Colour of Home*, new edition. London: Frances Lincoln Children's Books.

Laird, E. (2017) *Welcome to Nowhere*. London: Macmillan Children's Books.

Laird, E. (2020) *A House Without Walls*. London: Macmillan Children's Books.

Milner, K. (2017) *My Name is Not Refugee*. Edinburgh: The Bucket List.

Naylor-Ballesteros, C. (2019) *The Suitcase*. London: Nosy Crow.

Rauf, O. (2018) *The Boy at the Back of the Class*. London: Orion Children's Books.

Sanna, F. (2016) *The Journey*. London: Flying Eye Books.

Non-fiction

Roberts, C. and Kai, H. (2016) *Refugees and Migrants (Children in Our World)*. London: Hodder and Stoughton.

Rosen, M. and Young, A. (2019) *Who Are Refugees and Migrants? What Makes People Leave Their Homes? And Other Big Questions*. London: Wayland.

Websites

British Red Cross www.redcross.org.uk/get-involved/teaching-resources/refugees-you-me-and-those-who-came-before

British Red Cross has downloadable resources and lesson plans for refugee week.

Save the Children www.savethechildren.org/us/what-we-do/emergency-response/refugee-children-crisis

Save the Children explains the world refugee crisis and has information about what a refugee is, including useful video clips.

The UN Refugee Agency www.unhcr.org/uk/teaching-about-refugees.html

The UN Refugee Agency has teaching materials for different ages including animations, class discussion sheets and other activities about refugees.

16

Margaret Is From a Gypsy Family

My name is Margaret and I live in a caravan with my mum and dad and two older brothers. My brothers stopped going to school ages ago as they hated it so much and now they're happy helping my dad with his work. But I do want to go to school as I love reading and writing stories. My last teacher was nice and used to talk to me about books at break time when I was on my own, but then I had to leave the school as we were moving again. The problem is that we're *always* moving, so I never get settled in school and find it hard to make friends. This time we moved to a common just outside the town. There's no bus stop there so we have to walk, but it's not too far.

Last night we hardly slept as some people from the estate began to throw stones at our caravan and even broke two of the windows. My mum and dad had to get up in the night to put some cardboard in the windows to keep out the rain. Despite that, my mum got us all up early so I would be ready in really good time for school. She had ironed my skirt and laid out the shiny new shoes she'd bought especially for my big day. She brushed my hair until it shone, tied it up in a pink ribbon and told me how pretty I looked. I felt happy for a moment but that didn't help me with the sick feeling in my stomach at the thought of meeting all these new children. Mum couldn't take me to school as she had to see to the windows, but my brother took me to the end of the road where the school is. It had stopped raining and I could hear lots of birds singing and the happy sound of children playing.

I began to wonder, "Will it be okay this time?" Then, just before the school gate I saw two of the boys who had thrown the stones at our caravan. My heart sank. I looked down and walked faster but they started to shout at me loudly:

"Yeeuch!! Look who's coming, Dean. It's that kid from the caravans!"

Then the other boy yelled, "I see her, Liam. Let's get her!! Come on! Get moving!! Let's get her!" And then shouted at me, "Hey, pikey. What are you doing here? You don't belong in this town!"

They charged towards me, grabbed at my ribbon and pushed me into a puddle. They laughed their heads off!! I could see that they were going to hit me next and there were two of them against just me. One thing I am very good at and that's running. I even ran for charity at my last school. I got out of that puddle at top speed and kicked the smaller one. Then I ran as fast as I could through the school gate with these boys charging after me yelling nasty names. By now my shoes were all muddy and my hair was tangled and I looked a right mess.

Everyone stared at me. The teacher on duty didn't notice what had happened as it was all so sudden. No one came to help me.

The bell rang at that moment and we all went into our classes. I have never felt so sad in my life. What an awful start to my first day at school.

DEAN AND THE CARAVAN SITE

My name is Dean and I live on an estate with my mum and Mack, my older brother. Dad left last year but that was good as they were always arguing and fighting. I hate my big brother. He thinks now that Dad's gone he can beat me up whenever he likes. His nickname is Mack the Knife. I want to be as strong as he is when I grow up. Mum doesn't care about us any more since Dad left. One good thing though is that me and my friend Liam can stay out as late as we want and she never bothers.

Yesterday, just as it was getting dark, we had a great laugh. We went up to the common and broke some windows in the caravans. All these angry people came rushing out and chased us, but Liam and I got away easily.

This morning, the first kid we saw on the way to school was a girl from the caravans. I thought, "One of them coming to our school!! That's not on!! We'd better tell her who belongs here and who doesn't." We managed to get her down on the ground but then she jumped up and ran off. Liam is really mad at her as she kicked him hard, so he will be waiting for her on the way home tonight. We might get some other kids from the estate to join us.

TEACHER'S NOTES

Lesson objectives

⋄ To introduce pupils to the issue of ethnic minority Gypsy, Roma and Traveller people and to help them to understand something about their history and culture.

⋄ To encourage children to feel empathy for other children who have come to a new school and may feel anxious about how to make friends there.

Fact file
Definitions

Gypsy, Roma and *Traveller* communities are minority ethnic groups that have contributed to British society for centuries. Their distinctive way of life and traditions manifest themselves in nomadism, the centrality of their extended family, unique languages and entrepreneurial economy. Romany Gypsies are recognized as a separate ethnic group for the purposes of the Equality Act 2010 (and from before 1 October 2010 for the purposes of the Race Relations Act 1976). Irish Travellers are also recognized as a separate racial group. A person will be defined as a Romany Gypsy or Irish Traveller as a result of being born or marrying into a traditional Romany, Gypsy or Irish Traveller family. Furthermore, contrary to popular belief, three-quarters of Gypsy, Roma and Traveller families in the UK now live in settled accommodation; only a minority are itinerant. Local authorities have a duty to eradicate unlawful discrimination and to consider the effect of any proposed policies on ethnic minorities.

The impact of prejudice on children's education

In 2019, the Traveller Movement published a report *The Last Acceptable Form of Racism* that provided research evidence about the extent of segregation, bullying and discrimination experienced by Gypsy, Roma and Traveller families. According to this report, in school settings, teachers frequently overlook episodes of bullying against the children from these families and, in fact, often reinforce the stereotypes. Only four out of ten parents would be happy for their child to play with a Gypsy, Roma or Traveller classmate. Many of these children drop out of school rather than face daily discrimination. Children of Gypsy, Roma and Traveller families have the lowest attainment of all ethnic groups in the UK. Only a very few go to university.

In the story, Margaret's brothers hated their experience of school and dropped out as soon as they could to help their dad in his work. By contrast, Margaret is a bright, courageous girl who wants very much to go to school but, because of frequent moves by her family, she finds it hard to settle at school and has mixed feelings about her first day there. Unfortunately, her worst fears are realized when she is attacked by three boys from her class.

Comprehension activities

1. How does Margaret feel as she nears the school gate?

2. How will her parents feel when she tells them about her experience?

3. What do you think happened next?

Further activities

1. In pairs discuss how Margaret feels when she is attacked by the three boys. Discuss how she feels when no one helps her. Why do you think the other children did not help her? Why does Dean dislike Gypsy, Roma or Traveller families when they move near to his estate?

2. Make a plan. What sort of action could other children take when they see Margaret being pushed to the ground? Is there a peer support scheme in your school? How might peer supporters help her? In small groups, draw a picture showing ways in which peer supporters might help Margaret.

3. Mindfulness exercise – Travelling to a New Place: The Island. Sitting in a circle, the children are asked to close their eyes and breathe calmly and slowly for a minute or two. Then the teacher asks them to imagine that they are going on a long journey in a sailing boat. They travel over the sea. The teacher asks the children to imagine what they can see – the sun reflecting on the sea, little clouds in the sky, white crests of waves, land in the distance, sea birds – and hear – waves lapping against the side of the boat, birds calling, the wind in the sails. The land seems to come closer. The boat sails up to a sandy beach and they have landed. The teacher asks the children, still with their eyes closed, to look around the island. What do they see? What are the colours on the island? Are there trees there? Can they see and hear birds? Are there rocks? When they look down into the sea, are there strange, colourful fish there? The children walk along the sandy beach. They see some friendly animals on the beach. What do they look like? What colour are they? Are they big or small? Ask the children to imagine they reach out to stroke one of them. How does that feel? Is their fur rough or smooth? You see two children playing on the beach who look up and smile at you. You cannot understand what they are saying. They show you some

fruit hanging down from the tree. They reach up and take the fruit down and offer it to you. How does it taste? How do you thank them? They ask you to join their game. What are they doing? You join them. It is fun.

But now the sun is setting. It is time to go back. The teacher asks the children to get back into the boat and begin the journey home. On the journey the children are asked to think about the memories they will take back home with them and the stories they will tell their friends about the lovely island and the new friends they made there. The teacher lets the children know that they have come back to their classroom. She says, "We will return another day to your wonderful stories but right now we are going to let them go. Now you are going to breathe in, and when you breathe out, just blow your story away. When you have blown your story away, please open your eyes."

She then continues, "Now you are happy to be back in the classroom with the others that you know. While I count to five, look around and see how many eyes you can smile into. Now that I have counted to five, smile into my eyes and then we can go on to our next activity."

4. Make a poster. Design a colourful poster showing different ways of making a new pupil welcome in the class.

RESOURCES

Book

Mosley, J. (2000) *More Quality Circle Time*, 2nd edition. Wisbech, UK: LDA.

Websites

Amnesty International www.amnesty.org

Amnesty International reports regularly on the segregation, bullying and fear experienced by so many Gypsy, Traveller and Roma children throughout Europe. For example, in many European countries Roma children remain trapped in a cycle of poverty and marginalization. Roma children are disproportionately placed in schools for children with learning difficulties and in mainstream schools they often face bullying and harassment resulting in many of these children simply refusing to go back to school, so hindering their future opportunities in the wider society.

Anti-Bullying Alliance (ABA) www.anti-bullyingalliance.org.uk

The ABA summarizes the key recommendations from the Women and Equalities Committee report and provides useful links to their extensive range of anti-bullying interventions and policies. The ABA also has links to resource packs specifically designed to address the issue, including *Out of Site: Challenging Racism Towards Gypsy, Roma and Travellers*, an Education Pack from Show Racism the Red Card and reports, including *The Last Acceptable Form of Racism?* produced by the Traveller Movement.

Federation of Gypsy Liaison Groups and Anglia Ruskin University www.upr-info.org/sites/default/files/document/united_kingdom/session_27_-_may_2017/nfglg_upr27_gbr_e_main.pdf

This 2019 report on their collaborative research documents the finding that nine out of ten Gypsy, Roma or Traveller children in the UK have suffered racial abuse. Two-thirds have also been bullied or physically attacked and many are too scared to go to school.

Friends, Families and Travellers www.gypsy-traveller.org

This organization reports on several studies that confirm the extent to which Gypsy and Traveller children and young people are bullied more than any other ethnic minority in the UK. For example, one report, *Prejudice and Pride* by Jake Bowers, commissioned by Ormiston Children and Families Trust, documents the opinions of Traveller children in Cambridge about the issues that concern them. These young people reported that they had been bullied within the school system, physically assaulted in the community, had their caravans stoned and been spat on in public. Only 52 per cent of those interviewed said that they went to school, and 60 per cent felt that their culture was insufficiently valued and defended by schools. Prejudice towards Gypsy, Roma and Traveller children continues to be accepted in many quarters, and sections of the media create and then exacerbate moral panics among their readers about Gypsy, Roma and Traveller communities. This makes rational discussion about the issue extremely difficult.

Friends, Families and Travellers has a newsletter and a range of publications.

Parliament Select Committee www.parliament.uk

A report published in 2019 by the Women and Equalities Committee, House of Commons, chaired by MP Maria Miller, reports that Gypsy and Traveller people are likely to die a decade earlier than non-Travellers. Children from Gypsy or Roma backgrounds and those from a Traveller or Irish Heritage background have the lowest attainment of all ethnic groups throughout their school years (according to the Government Race Disparity Audit) and only a handful of their young people go to university every year. Many Roma are exploited by rogue landlords and paid far below the minimum wage. Although three out of four Gypsies and Travellers live in settled accommodation, government policy is overwhelmingly focused on planning and encampments to the extent that a wide range of policy making around such issues as education and service provision is ignored. As Maria Miller writes:

Gypsy, Roma and Traveller people have been comprehensively failed by policy makers and public services for too long. Access to education, health, employment, criminal justice, tackling hate crime and domestic violence – all these require services which differentiate between different groups who have different needs, and yet so many services are ill-equipped to support Gypsy, Roma and Traveller people. The Government must stop filing this under "too difficult" and set out how it intends to improve health, education and other outcomes for these very marginalized communities who are all too often "out of sight and out of mind."

A parent who submitted evidence to the Committee said:

My daughter has been called names at her secondary school because it is known that she is a Gypsy. Horrible names. I want her to stay there but it is hard. Teachers don't take it seriously enough. They might say to the child to apologize but that's not enough. Any other racism in the school is taken up higher.

The Traveller Movement www.travellermovement.org.uk

This is a charity that is committed to the fulfilment of human rights for ethnic minority Gypsy, Roma and Traveller people.

Cassie Marie McDonagh, herself an Irish Traveller, has written a book *I'm Not Allowed to Play with You Anymore* (2017) that vividly illustrates Gypsy and Traveller children's experiences of being bullied and socially excluded at school, which can be downloaded from https://travellermovement.org.uk/wp-content/uploads/book1e-FINAL-WEB.pdf

Epilogue

In the Garden

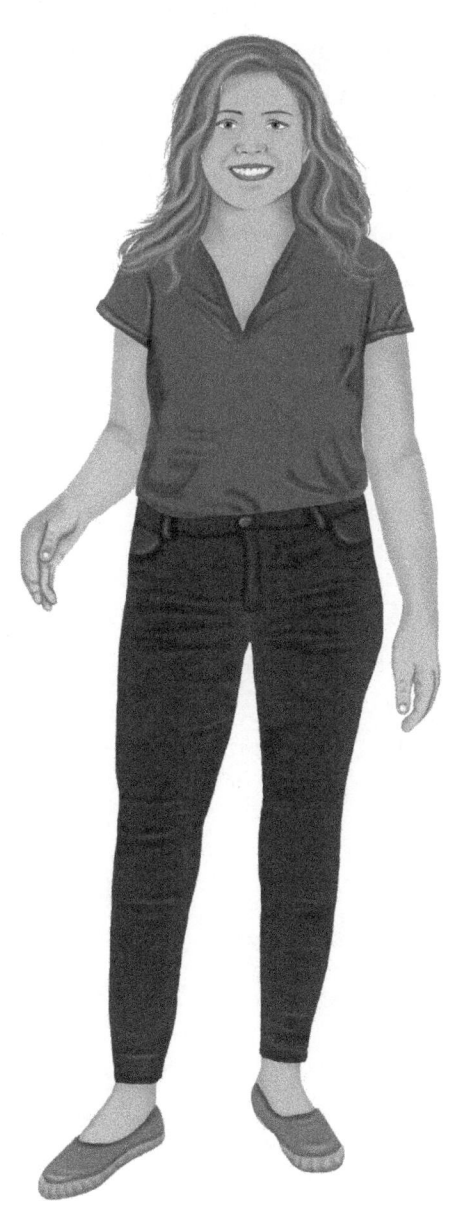

It was the last day of the summer term. The weather was perfect. The whole class was celebrating in the eco garden they had all worked so hard to create. They had gathered the vegetables and piled a big bowl full of strawberries. The marigolds and nasturtiums were in full bloom. Some huge sunflowers towered above the children, each one grown from seed.

"Look how far we've come!" said Mrs Davies. "We've grown together, just like this lovely garden. Don't forget that the garden grew out of your worries about the environment in the wider world!"

The class looked around at all the flowers and plants and felt proud of what they had achieved. They realized how many skills they had learnt and how they had worked together as a team.

"We have had our ups and downs," Mrs Davies continued. "Some of you had problems in your families; some of you sadly suffered a bereavement; some of you worried about the way you look or your gender; we had some bullying and cyberbullying; we fell out with our friends and then made up; some new people joined our class and we found ways to make them welcome. Through all this, we have learnt to understand each other better, and realize how we all experience the world differently. And we have shown how important it is to help one another when things get difficult, as they do for all of us at times. I am so proud of you! Your journey will carry on next year when you will grow even stronger together. Please come to see me and tell me how you're getting on.

"I will miss you all."

Index